DIRTY
─Sexy─
POLITICS
★

MEGHAN MCCAIN

DIRTY
—Sexy—
POLITICS

HYPERION

NEW YORK

Library of Congress Cataloging-in-Publication Data has been
applied for.

ISBN 978-1-4013-2377-6

Hyperion books are available for special promotions and premi-
ums. For details contact the HarperCollins Special Markets De-
partment in the New York office at 212-207-7528, fax 212-207-7222,
or e-mail spsales@harpercollins.com.

Book design by Shubhani Sarkar

FIRST EDITION

10   9   8   7   6   5   4   3   2   1

THIS LABEL APPLIES TO TEXT STOCK

We try to produce the most beautiful books possible, and we are
also extremely concerned about the impact of our manufacturing
process on the forests of the world and the environment as a whole.
Accordingly, we've made sure that all of the paper we use has been
certified as coming from forests that are managed to ensure the
protection of the people and wildlife dependent upon them.

FOR MY PARENTS,
WHO TAUGHT ME TO LOVE LIFE.

CONTENTS

★

Contents

DIRTY
—Sexy—
POLITICS

★

Sex and politics are a lot alike.
You don't have to be good at them to enjoy them.

BARRY GOLDWATER

★

INTRODUCTION

FREEDOM IS ADDICTIVE. ONCE YOU'VE TASTED IT, YOU WILL HUNT FOR IT AGAIN AND AGAIN. AND OUR PASSION FOR FREEDOM BRINGS US TOGETHER more than it pulls us apart. We have fought to remove obstacles in the way of it—we have battled and died, picketed, paraded, rallied, and staked everything we've had on it. We founded our country with our desire for freedom and it continues to drive our nation's energy and progress.

I was raised in a house that was open to new ideas, new people, and open to our differences. We had rules about how to treat others, rules about being honest and respectful. We had rules about tolerance. But they weren't rules that were supposed to brainwash us and turn us into mini Cindy and John McCains. My brothers and sister and I were raised with a taste of freedom. My parents believed in us—believed in the people we were and the people we would become.

Would they really want me to have tattoos, swear on TV, or even write this book? Uhmmm. Maybe not. And that's the point. I am not a social or physical extension of my mom and dad—except that I represent their great hope that freedom, and room to grow, is how individuals find themselves and create their own lives. Under that big, wide-open sky of Arizona, where I grew up, there seemed to be room for everybody.

Honesty is a quality of freedom—and is addictive and exhilarating in the same way. By being honest about yourself, you are asking for room and space. You are making a declaration of your humanity and independence. If we are honest with ourselves and about ourselves, suddenly everybody has a little more room to be free. We are more trustworthy if we are honest, too. If we are open, we aren't hiding anything.

"There are no secrets" is one of my personal mottos. I feel that hiding is a waste of time and energy. Everybody will figure out what kind of human being you really are. So I like to save people the trouble and just lay it out there. *What you see is what you get.* But I do respect the fact that some people are more private by nature than I am.

Which is why, after writing a draft of this book, I took a step back and considered whether I had been too honest. Maybe I was making a mistake to share so many of the intimate details as I watched my dad run for president. Suddenly, it seemed scary to open the windows and let everybody see a snapshot of my life at a time when I was young, impressionable, and feeling a bit frantic. But the children of politicians have a surreal life and it was time somebody started talking about it.

Did I change any names to protect the innocent? Normally I don't like this kind of thing. But ultimately, I decided to protect the identities of a few campaign staffers and members of the media about whom I had bad things to say. I did not give my parents carte blanche to make changes, nor did my father's senate office have a look at the manuscript before it was published. So if you have a problem with the contents of this book, hold only me responsible.

In a few instances, nicknames are used. This is meant as a goodwill gesture. I am a work in progress—and embarrassed myself many times during the seventeen months that I was on the road with the campaign. I thought it would be only fair to give a few people the break I would hope they would give me.

Did I make stuff up? No. Apparently there is a long-standing tradition of making things up in a memoir so your life seems worse and better than it really was. I get it. There's a need for drama and good plot twists. But in the case of this book, I didn't make things up. As for plot twists, the whole world knows how this book ends already. My dad loses.

If events seem altered, it isn't intentional. It is how I remembered things. I checked dates and facts, and corroborated my accounts with friends and family, but my stories are decidedly impressionistic rather than reportorial. This is how I remember my time on my father's campaign.

Another thing this book doesn't do intentionally: score settling. Lots of political memoirs are written with an ax to grind. The embittered writer comes off like the wisest or folksiest person around and, if the world had just listened to her, everything would have been fantastic. Well, I really hope that this book isn't like that.

I am not a politician trying to drum up support. I have no plans to ever run for office. My hope is to present a unique account of history without compromising it with attempts to make myself look really good. I turned twenty-three and twenty-four while on the road campaigning and, as you will see, my age and inexperience showed.

I don't have a secret agenda, in other words, aside from wanting to be honest, entertaining, and also insightful about a particularly interesting election in our nation's history. My hope is that this book will encourage readers to become involved in the democratic process—and look at politics in a new way. If I'm totally honest with myself, the only score that I may be trying to settle is one with the Republican Party, which seems to have lost its way in the last ten years.

I realize that it is ironic that this book tells the story of my own struggle to get my act together. But it is one of the bizarre realities of life that you can be a mess yourself but still see so clearly what is wrong with others.

I used to joke that I am hooked on "taking the red pill," a reference to the science fiction movie *The Matrix* in which the main character, Neo, is "taking the red pill" and choosing to face the reality of the Matrix—rather than "taking the blue pill" and wanting to believe in a lie. When I meet somebody new, I will sometimes say, "He's taking the blue pill." This means he is living in a dream world.

Here's my dream: The political party that identifies with the color red should start taking pills of the same color.

Honesty. Individualism. Freedom. Back in the day, these concepts were the bedrock of the Republican Party. It wasn't that long ago, either. I am old enough to remember Barry Goldwater, the late senator from Arizona. He was a great conservative visionary, a man of great charm and a playful spirit. As a little girl, I remember goofing around with him. Once, when he and I were having our picture taken together, I stuck my tongue out at him. Without a moment's pause, Senator Goldwater stuck out his tongue at me right back.

Like my dad, Barry Goldwater had an independent spirit. He was a natural leader and natural politician. And even though he ran for president and lost, the principles that he stood for endured and inspired a generation of conservatives who followed him. He believed passionately in freedom and protecting the rights of the individual— ideas that became fundamental to Ronald Reagan twenty years later, and would lead to his success. Goldwater's lifelong crusade against groupthink and the expansion of federal government continue to be relevant today, as we wonder where the Obama bailouts and big programs will take us and our country.

I love the ideas of Barry Goldwater, and what he left behind. Yes, his vision was anti–big government, but even more than that, it was pro-people and pro-freedom. He believed in making room and space for individuals to live their own lives, and create relationships and families and businesses with as little interference from others as possible.

It was about removing fences, not building them. It was about tolerance. It was about appreciating differences and new ideas. He was called "Mr. Conservative," and in Goldwater's dream for America, and the one he fought for his entire life, there was room for everybody to flourish.

These days, the name Ronald Reagan—as well as his legacy—has become oversaturated, just white noise. Conservatives love to evoke him, using him as an example of whatever brand of politics they happen to be selling. But what they seem to have forgotten is that moderates and Democrats elected Ronald Reagan, not the Far Right. The ideas that he stood for—freedom, the individual, and self-reliance—appealed to a broad political spectrum. He believed that it was our independent spirit and our differences that made this country great.

I have to wonder, if he and Goldwater were alive today and could see where their party has gone in the last decade, what they would think. Somehow the walls closed in. The conservative movement seems hell-bent on constricting our freedoms rather than expanding them. The base has moved to the Far Right and, sadly, it seems to be dying there.

Rather than the party of openness and individual freedom, it is now the party of limited message and less freedom. Along with an ideological narrowness, an important PR battle is being lost. Rather than leading us into the exhilarating fresh air of liberty, a chorus of voices on the radical right is taking us to a place of intolerance and anger. We hear them on the radio and TV. They love to spread fear because it keeps the money rolling in. You know who I'm talking about. The more afraid we are, the richer they get.

If they have their way, we will be scared all the time, particularly of ideas that seem new, or foreign, or different, even if they are great ideas, even if they are in support of freedom.

Rather than being the party of limitless freedom and rejection of groupthink, they want the Republican Party to become a private club. Not everybody is allowed in, or invited. If you don't hold the accepted attitudes, you don't fit in. You are called a RINO, or "Republican in Name Only."

That's what they call me, in fact—as if I haven't earned the right to be included in the party.

But why?

If not me, who?

Would Barry Goldwater and Ronald Reagan be RINOs too?

Somehow, being a Republican isn't a political decision anymore. It is a lifestyle choice. You have to look one way, think one way, and act one way. Wear the uniform! Embrace groupthink! And for goodness' sake, no strangers allowed! Somehow it is wrong to consider modern life and the complications and innovations and changes the last thirty years have brought. The doors and windows aren't just shut. The curtains are drawn.

Let's open the windows! I don't like private clubs or secrets or living in a bubble world. Let's honor our differences, and different lifestyles, even celebrate them. With this book, I hope to bring some fresh air into the room, maybe knock down a few walls. I wouldn't mind crashing through the ceiling, too. Let the sky open up, and freedom ring. Hey everybody, come on in!

I

HOW THINGS WENT BADLY

THE NIGHT BEFORE IT WAS ANNOUNCED THAT SARAH PALIN WOULD BE MY FATHER'S RUNNING MATE FOR VICE PRESIDENT, I WENT TO SLEEP joking with Shannon and Heather about what it would be like campaigning across the country with five married Mormon men and all those baby grandchildren of Mitt Romney. My roommates and I had lots of jokes about the Romneys, who seemed doomed to join the campaign any second. They were all so handsome, in a tooth-whitener commercial kind of way, and so seriously wholesome. We wondered whether the Five Brothers, the nickname for the Romney sons, could handle the constant drinking and swearing that went on in our campaign—the press corps included. Not to mention all the tawdry stories about crazy-sex that you never read about.

Crazy-sex, in case some clarification is necessary, is a category of sex on its own. It is sex with somebody who is extremely bad for you. Somebody you probably don't even like that much. But on the road, things have a way of changing. You don't have regular contact with friends. You don't see your family that often. You start to miss them both, and your comfortable bed at home. This causes you to look at the world differently, through what we called "campaign goggles." It was just like "beer goggles," when people around you seem more fascinating the more you drink, except it's caused by prolonged contact. Each day of togetherness on a campaign, stuck on a bus or airplane, listening to one more stump speech, brought you closer and closer until, very slowly over time, even the most boring campaign drones and journalists started to seem attractive. Campaign goggles can distort reality very powerfully and are the cause of almost all crazy-sex and other campaign hookups.

Stories abound, and I'm sure you've heard some, about how wild and raucous and lusty political life can be, especially during a presidential election. When the stakes are high, the behavior gets really low. I don't want to give the impression that I'm immune to bad behavior. But while my father was making a bid for the presidency, I didn't have a death wish—which meant absolutely, positively, no crazy-sex for me. It was the kind of decision that has "SURVIVAL SKILLS" written all over it.

The night before the announcement, I had a nice big king-sized bed all to myself. It was late and I was having trouble settling down. I swilled Red Bull and Diet Coke all day on the campaign, gorged on pizza and donuts, and at night, after all that sugar and caffeine, it was hard to decompress. Shannon and Heather—my friends, angels, and colleagues who took videos and still photographs for the campaign and my blog—were in an adjoining room. I could hear them laughing. On the road, we were always together, our days spent mostly in transit, on one of the three campaign buses that took everybody around the country. At night, we shared connecting rooms in Holiday Inns—very rarely anything nicer. One room had a king. The next room had two twins. We always took turns getting our own room.

When I finished college, I told my parents that I didn't want to go to graduate school, or open a clothing boutique, as previously discussed. I wanted to join the campaign. They said that I could come along if I paid my own way. The campaign was a sinking ship, or at least financially sunk, when I joined in July 2007. There was no money for extras, and no money for me, or my blog, or the people I'd need to help me produce it. My father's campaign manager, Terry Nelson, and the campaign strategist, John Weaver—who was one of my father's closest friends, and like an uncle to me—had run the operation into near bankruptcy. Poll numbers were slipping. Fund-raising had stalled. Our spirits were low and it was hard to be optimistic, but my dad wasn't resigned to another loss.

And neither was I. I would do anything for him, and relished the thought of a front row seat on the campaign. To bankroll myself and the blog, I used the money that my grandfather had left me, even if, by the end, I had spent every dime. It was a better education than graduate school and more worthwhile to me than opening a boutique. As far as I could tell, the Republican Party was hopelessly unschooled in lots of things, but particularly in its efforts to attract young people by using the Internet, in spite of all the millions of dollars spent on "web consulting."

By being independent, and not paid for by the McCain campaign, I'd be free to write what I wanted—or so I hoped—while revealing a more personal side of my dad and my family (the campaign, for all its experts and big thinkers, seemed particularly bad at this). But my blog had led to conflicts, a big ugly mess of them.

IN MY HEART OF HEARTS, I'D ALWAYS HOPED MY FATHER would pick Senator Joe Lieberman as his running mate. Aside from being a brilliant politician, Joe is one of the kindest, friendliest, and funniest people I have ever met, not particularly common traits when it comes to the famous and powerful. Always in good spirits, he never seems affected by the fray, or criticism. Sometimes his jokes alone kept me sane during those endless bus rides throughout the country.

Probably even more important, Joe Lieberman is one of the people whom my father can relax around—always. For me, this counts for a lot. Like everything else in my life, the personal and the professional are hard to pull apart, and usually I don't want to. If I like somebody enough to be friends with them, that's exactly the kind of person I want to work with.

Politically speaking, picking Lieberman seemed like a brilliant move too. He is a former Democrat, and was previously the running mate of Al Gore. I have to admit, I loved the idea of having two independent-leaning politicians on the Republican ticket against the steadily left-leaning Barack Obama. I thought this would pull moderates like me—there were thirty million or more of us floating around the country—in the party's direction.

But by the time I went to bed on the night of August 28, 2008, I had already been told that Joe Lieberman and Bobby Jindal, the governor of Louisiana, hadn't made the final cut. That left me assuming—to the point of certainty—that Mitt Romney, the former governor of Massachusetts, would be chosen. There was a slight possibility it could be Tim Pawlenty, who had a great head of hair. But aside from this fact, and that he was the governor of Minnesota, I knew nothing else about him.

My focus had been on Romney for months. He was a minor obsession of mine, I have to confess—the politician whom I most loved to watch and ridicule during the primaries. He'd given me so many sublime moments of laughter. It was incredible how he kept switching his story, and backpedaling, and making my father out to be an old has-been and tired Washington insider.

YouTube had an irresistible Romney clip that we'd all seen and laughed over. It showed a heated squabble between the governor and a chubby, semi-dorky AP reporter named Glenn Johnson at a press conference inside a Staples office supply store. Johnson is rumpled and sitting on the floor of Staples, legs stretched out, his laptop attached to him like a college student. Romney is standing over him, super-erect, his hair gelled and perfectly black. He's wearing a plaid shirt and a Windbreaker, and like so many of Romney's "spontaneous" moments on his campaign, he seems so unnatural.

From his spot on the floor, Glenn Johnson keeps drilling away with questions about Romney hiring Washington lobbyists on his campaign, while Romney becomes more and more frustrated.

Romney's campaign manager eventually loses it, and pulls the reporter aside. "Don't be argumentative with the candidate!" It's truly priceless, and I loved how Romney, who always came off as slick and unreal, had been undone by such a visual mess of a guy. I'd seen the clip at least fifty times and laughed every time. (Much later, I ran into Glenn Johnson on the street in New York and told him how much I loved his YouTube clip. For the record, he'd lost an extreme amount of weight by then and looked great.)

It was hard to adjust to nice thoughts about Romney—or to stop laughing at him. But that's politics. You could loathe somebody during the primaries and then, suddenly, consider him a good guy and shrewd politician as soon as you've beaten him and he's joined your team. Just a few months earlier, Romney's campaign and ours were intense rivals. But now that we were supposed to be the best of friends, I needed to put jokes aside and focus on the tremendous positives Romney would bring to the ticket. He was handsome, smart, and extremely experienced in matters of the economy, an issue that would eventually become lethal to my father's campaign. Also, I had met the governor and some of his campaign operatives and have to admit that they were a lot more easygoing and real than I ever thought possible.

Let's be honest. We needed Mitt Romney. He made perfect sense. We could put down the sword because, at the end of the day, we were fighting for the same political ideals. We were all Republicans—and fought for individual freedom, smaller government, a strong defense. These ideals were things that we cared passionately about, and were supposed to be more important than cultural or religious divides, more important than what kind of clothes we wore, or whether we had sex before marriage—or even whom we had sex with.

That's how it was supposed to be, anyway. But increasingly, the more conservative wing of the Republican Party wasn't accepting of moderates like me. It wasn't enough that we all shared a conservative philosophy that we cared passionately about. It seemed like you had to prove you were *conservative enough.* It made me uneasy. And, like all humor, my jokes about Romney shielded something very real. It wasn't so much that I disapproved of the Romneys. I worried they'd disapprove of me—my bleached hair, my swearing, my "edgy" clothes, not to mention my gay friends. Would they accept me or scorn me as some kind of closet liberal who didn't fit in?

Being a Republican was sometimes difficult if you had any wayward ideas or attitudes, or if your lifestyle wasn't conventional—even though what was "conventional" had eroded to the point of being unrecognizable, or didn't exist anymore. Republicans seemed to yearn for the golden era of the Reagan eighties, when AIDS wasn't discussed, along with so many other things. Now, in an effort to pretend nothing had changed, the party seemed like a secret sect, a membership that you had to prove yourself worthy of.

But what about the less "conventional" people who hated groupthink and just wanted to live life without big government breathing down our backs? And what about me? I am passionate about individual liberty. I believe in God and the church, but am as adamantly pro-life as I am passionate in my support of gay marriage. What worried me much more than the Romneys or Huckabees disapproving of me personally—I could deal with that—was how moderates like me would ever fit into their idea of what a Republican was, or should be. With these exclusionary attitudes, in ten or twenty years there would be no party left.

But it was too soon to go down this road. We'd given up a shot at Joe Lieberman, and had most likely moved on to Mitt Romney. This would bring changes to our Pirate Ship, as our campaign was lovingly called. We'd have to clean up our act a little bit. Not that I really drank much, or ever took drugs. And I was celibate as a nun. But I suspected my days of swearing like a sailor and dancing in the bus aisles were over.

The future was full of unknowns. But I had learned a few things on the campaign already, and knew that change always brought complications and chaos—and sometimes a little entertainment. Drama was inevitable on a campaign and created almost out of thin air. Tempers were always flying, and feelings were always being hurt. There was no question that a running mate would add to the confusion and upset. There would be less time for fun. But I couldn't have predicted just how serious it was going to get.

2

THE SUSPENSE WASN'T KILLING ME

I WAS DEAD ASLEEP WHEN I HEARD THE TELEVISION CLICK ON IN THE NEXT ROOM. SHANNON AND HEATHER WERE IN THEIR TWIN BEDS, AND I RE-member waking up with a jolt and yelling out, "Is Romney on TV yet?"

Silence.

I heard the voice of Dana Bash, the correspondent on CNN, giving a report. But the exact words were garbled.

The suspense should have killed me, but it hadn't—not yet, anyway. I do remember having extreme anxiety as soon as I woke up and feeling, suddenly, very angry that I still had no idea who my father's running mate was. It was mystifying how unplugged-in I was. It was galling, and seemed a little crazy, that I, the candidate's daughter and a campaign blogger, had no idea whether I would be campaigning tomorrow with Romney, Pawlenty, or some random politician I'd never met.

"Is it Romney?" I called out louder.

They didn't know, they said. It wasn't part of the broadcast.

"How can that be possible?"

Why didn't Dana Bash know? Dana always knew—always—what

was going on. She was the CNN correspondent on the campaign and a very classy one, actually one of the very few journalists I always enjoyed being around because she respected the concept of "off the record."

Still in bed, and in my pajamas, I grabbed my cell phone from the nightstand and called my mother.

"Mom, who is it?"

She paused.

"Mom, *do you know?*"

"I'm not going to tell you," she said.

"What!?"

"We don't want anyone to know."

Now, let me say my mother and I have a very open relationship. She has stuck by me, defended me, nurtured and supported me. Aside from some dorky outfits she used to put on me when I was little, she has never tried to meld me into her clone. Ever since I can remember, she has been my biggest, most loyal cheerleader. We've had our ups and downs, like any mother and daughter, but we worked through things by talking. Communication was essential. But that morning, she let me down.

To make matters worse, my dad clearly had a hand in the decision to cut me out too.

I clicked off the phone and immediately started crying. Crying became bawling, which evolved quickly into uncontrollable sobbing. I am sensitive, way too sensitive for politics probably, and really emotional by nature. I can't fight it and I don't want to. I'd rather have big feelings than shut down and become dead inside. I've seen what that way of dealing with life does to people, how it plays a direct hand in the disconnection between politics and people.

Shannon and Heather surrounded me. You couldn't ask for better friends. They tried to console me and at the same time, make me get in the shower because I was going to have to be onstage that day, in just a few hours, and stand alongside my father and mother and the new, wrongfully secret, vice presidential running mate.

Shannon tried to keep things light. "You need to bathe!"

I kept sobbing.

"You've got to pull it together!"

I was still overcome.

"People are going to be watching you, girl."

It was hard to fathom why my parents would let me down so much.

"Get showered, get serious, and get some mascara on!"

Eventually, I ended up getting in the shower, but couldn't find the will—or whatever it takes—to wash my hair. I know in the scheme of things it doesn't matter, and it won't say on my tombstone, HAD DIRTY HAIR WHEN SHE MET SARAH PALIN, but girls, you know those mornings, and you know the feeling. What was I thinking? Why didn't I take the time to shampoo? Not to mention that part of my job—as daughter-of and political prop—is to have clean hair, but I'd already failed at that.

Next, I had to decide what to wear, just as my bags were being taken away.

I should explain. Presidential campaigns have something called "bag call." We had to pack and leave our suitcases outside our hotel rooms ninety minutes before departing for the day's events. It sounds so organized and tidy. But in reality, it's a giant pain in the ass. There were often things that I needed to get ready in the morning—my cosmetics and toiletries, to start with. If I didn't get showered and dressed well ahead of schedule, I would have to pull out everything I thought I'd need that day before surrendering my suitcase. The result was that I, like most of the women on the campaign, lugged around a giant purse or tote bag with my pajamas and toiletries in it, or whatever hadn't made it into my suitcase by the time the advance team took them away.

That morning, knowing that bag call was imminent, I rushed to my suitcase and began pulling out things that would look good on-stage. I rummaged and rummaged—sometimes it was just a challenge to find anything that was clean—and eventually pulled out a black cotton Theory dress. I'm not sure why I picked it, except that it was black and, since I was dealing with campaign weight gain, it fit.

I put on the Theory dress, pulled my hair back into a ponytail, and I started sliding toward another emotional crash, thinking about how I still didn't know who the running mate was and that, on a day so important, I was going to look like a hot mess.

Shannon and Heather were glued to CNN, waiting for the an-nouncement. As soon as I emerged from the bathroom, Shannon shot me a look. "Don't you have anything *else* to wear?"

"I thought there was a rule about cotton and linen," Heather said.

It's true. There *is* an unwritten rule, which I had always danger-ously ignored. I have been told that you shouldn't wear silk or linen or cotton onstage at a political rally. It's better to stick with knits. I never understood it, or even wanted to. But knits can withstand the heat of the stage lights and there is virtually no possibility of undergarments showing through in pictures. So the threat of embarrassments, like bra or thong exposure, is almost nil. Looking back, it explained why political women of both parties seemed to gravitate to the St. John knits uniform.

And yet, there I was, in black cotton.

It was a short dress too, and well above my knee.

Strung out, sleep deprived, and now panicked that I had made a tragic wardrobe mistake, I ran out into the hotel hallway to find an-other dress to wear. Tears began welling up in my eyes and rolling down my cheeks as I bent over my bulging suitcase and unzipped it. The contents spilled out onto the floor, underwear included.

At that very moment, two campaign staffers, Mr. Burns and Blond Amazon, walked by, carefully stepping away from me and my stuff. I despised both of them, which made this entire incident so much worse, and also is why I am not using their real names and will be sticking to nicknames for now.

I called one of them Mr. Burns due to his uncanny resemblance to the bald and very mean character on *The Simpsons*. But this only expresses a fraction of the contempt and disregard that I had for him. Mr. Burns was, and always will be, my least favorite person on the campaign. I know I will later claim that Steve Schmidt was my least favorite person on the campaign, but I really do mean it about Mr. Burns. My father loves him, so a protective cloud swirls around Mr. Burns. But I must say he is truly one of the most unpleasant people I have ever met.

An investment banker who joined the campaign temporarily and then never left, Mr. Burns was obsessed with control and access and took great pride in being on the inside. He kept a very tight grip on his various power centers, but his main concern seemed to be the seating arrangements for the passenger vans and the three campaign buses— aka the Straight Talk Express.

Mr. Burns expressed his feelings about you by your placement on a particular bus. The first bus, where my mom and dad rode, was the nicest by far—luxurious leather seats, clean and comfortable, stocked with potato chips and Diet Cokes, and driven by the amazing Jay Frye, who leaned down from his height of six foot five to give me a huge hug every time he saw me. The second bus was loaded with important media and plugged-in staffers. The air was heavy, the talk intelligent, the atmosphere was urgent and intense, no-nonsense and only occasionally outrageous. And then there was the third bus, which was old and rank-smelling, populated by hair and makeup people, insignificant media or out-of-favor ones, campaign surrogates that nobody wanted to deal with, and an assortment of other disenfranchised types who seemed lonely and forgotten. It was like the Island of Misfit Toys.

I'll confess, I always tried to get along with Mr. Burns, hoping for a better place on the bus, hoping that he'd let me bring Shannon and Heather into the first bus so we could ride with my parents. I was

loyal to my friends and refused to sit on the first bus without them—
something that kept me from riding in official motorcades and caused
me to get left behind at quite a few places. But increasingly, it was
hard to be fake-nice to Mr. Burns. To me, he had become a cartoon.

Blond Amazon was my nickname for the other staffer who was
walking down the corridor that morning, a super-tall and aggressively
blond woman, as you might suspect, who exuded a one-of-the-guys
toughness on a daily basis during the campaign. I have a very good
relationship with her now—I adore her, essentially, and she has become
more supportive of me—but during the campaign, probably due to the
stressed-out environment that made me feel threatened and negative all
the time, I loathed her passionately, dreaded seeing her, and sometimes referred to my clashes with her as "Another Attack of the Fifty-
Foot Woman."

Making matters worse, Secret Service agents would sometimes
confuse me with Blond Amazon at rallies, which I found more annoying than I can say—particularly since she is a foot taller than I am.
What kind of recruitment and training is going on, anyway, when a
Secret Service agent can't distinguish two blond women who are a foot
apart in height?

And there she was, the invincible Amazon, striding down the corridor with Mr. Burns.

I was crouching on the floor. My clothes and unmentionables were
strewn about, and I had my hands on several dresses—still worrying
about what to wear that day.

"Do you know *who it is?*" I blurted out.

Blurting might be the wrong word. It might have been somewhat
louder. I could have been screaming.

Advance guys were swarming around the halls by then, picking
up the suitcases and dealing with bag call. I started to gather up my
clothes and stuff them back into my suitcase.

Blond Amazon and Mr. Burns kept walking, like I was a phantom or an escapee from a nearby mental ward, which, at that point, I probably looked like.

"Do you know?" I insisted, a bit louder.

I don't remember the exact answer, if there was one. My actual memory is that they just walked on, neither of them truly acknowledging me, like I was roadkill that you drive by without braking for a better look.

Mr. Burns signaled to me, finally, that he knew who the running mate was. He nodded, or winked. He might have made a hand gesture. More than anything, he communicated that he was enjoying the fact that he knew and I didn't.

Overcome with fury, I yelled out, "Screw you both!!" then grabbed a black knit dress and flew inside my hotel room. With the door safely closed, I lost it—to the point of wailing. My own bad behavior made me feel worse, as it always did. There was no escaping the reality of my incredibly rude and inappropriate screaming in the hallway, as witnessed by more people than I care to think about, particularly two people whom I disliked with unimaginable intensity. *Screw you both!*

All I wanted in life was to be important enough, and trusted enough, to know who my father's running mate was.

Was that too much to ask?

Had I been so untrustworthy, so spoiled and difficult?

The fact that my nemesis, Mr. Burns, the Bus Roster Nazi, was more inside and trusted, and more important . . . well, that really was the last kicker.

3

MEETING SARAH

SUDDENLY ON THE TV SCREEN, THERE WAS AN
ALERT ABOUT A PRIVATE PLANE FROM ALASKA
THAT HAD FLOWN INTO OHIO THAT MORNING AND
for the first time ever, I saw Sarah Palin's face. It flashed across the
screen, along with the news that she was the likely choice of running
mate. You remember the picture, the one of her in the red jacket with
the big smile? The pundits on television were pronouncing her name
wrong—saying "Pah-len" instead of "Pay-lin."

At that very moment, my mom appeared in my hotel room.

"Is that it? *Is she Dad's choice?*" I yelled.

My mom nodded. "Yes," she said, then told me to get ready as soon
as possible. "I love you. It's going to be fine. I'll explain everything
later."

I wanted to ask more questions, but a closer study of my mother's
face told me that she was as frustrated as I was. Grabbing my purse
and giant bag with my UGG boots and pajamas—my hotel room
uniform—as well as the knit dress that I had decided to change into

later, and all my toiletries and makeup, I headed to the parking lot with Shannon and Heather.

The bus roster for the day said it all: Mr. Burns had assigned me, Shannon, and Heather to the third bus, the one with the smallest bathroom and a smell so foul you kept wanting to open the windows, except there weren't any.

There was no fight left in me. We just got on, joined by random staffers I had barely met and my mother's hair and makeup people. I spoke to no one, just squeezed into the awful bathroom with my massive tote bag and, while the bus was rocking and weaving to our next destination, an Ohio high school where my father would present his running mate to the world, I tried to change dresses and get my hair into a tighter ponytail.

When a zipper became stuck on my bra, I kicked open the bathroom door, stood in the back of the bus in my bra, and called out to my friends. Modesty was an extravagance at that point, but I did try to turn away, allowing everybody on the bus to see the back of my bra. More than anything, I wanted to stop crying. I did deep breathing exercises, and focused on the next few hours to come—the TV cameras, the crowded auditorium, the faces to meet and greet, the commotion and excitement.

This nomination was meant to stir things up, rejuvenate support, throw the world a curveball, and sweep us to victory. The running mate announcement was the biggest turning point of any presidential campaign. I kept saying to myself, "Pull your shit together. Pull your shit together. You're about to meet Sarah Palin—*does it rhyme with Allen?*—and her family. This is an important moment in your life."

By the time I got off the bus, I was able to put on the fake smile that I was so good at, and follow my mom and all the staffers and advisers, our entire campaign entourage, as it paraded through the back door of a high school gym, and into its locker room, where a makeshift greenroom had been set up, with folding chairs and tables.

Blond Amazon motioned me to follow her. Behind a blue curtain were Sarah and Todd Palin, as well as Bristol, Willow, Piper, and Trig. My father came over and introduced us. I remember how cheerily I said, "Hi, I'm Meghan, such an honor to meet you! We're about to go on a great adventure together!"

"What an honor and privilege it is to be here," Sarah said—or words to that effect. She thanked my father, but soon enough the greetings were over and an uncomfortable silence fell over us, reminding me of a seventh-grade dance with everybody standing awkwardly around. It was as if, after the rehearsed niceties, it was too hard to move into anything real—or make more of an effort.

Outside, beyond the blue curtain, past the stage and audience, journalists were assembled on risers, along with dozens of cameras and microphones, waiting to record a few minutes of the introductions, which would, in turn, be cut down to a few seconds, a few snapshots and sound bites. What was the point of trying to say something real, anyway? And what was the hurry?

As I stood alongside the Palins, my first impressions of Sarah were that she was the most beautiful politician I had ever seen, that she seemed surprisingly calm, and that she had a ton of kids. She seemed all American, too, and I remember noticing how formally she addressed my father, calling him "sir." She was wearing a black suit with three-quarter sleeves and a cool pair of red patent leather peep-toe shoes. They were hip, even trendy. And I remember liking that. More than anything, I was excited by the fact that she was a woman, and with each passing minute the reality of this, and what it meant, not just for me, but for the country and the world, was sinking in. It wasn't only that she was a woman. She was such a beautiful one at that.

I loved the way she and my dad looked together—physically, I thought they complemented each other very well. There was also discussion about Sarah being a "maverick," something I thought we'd have in common.

But when I looked over at Bristol, who was holding her baby brother, Trig, I remember thinking two things: That poor girl looks shell-shocked and *why does she have a giant blanket covering her stomach?*

A new phase was dawning in our lives, and in the life of our campaign. I felt that too. The relationship between a presidential candidate and the running mate is extremely personal and intimate. In essence these two people and their two families become one family and one entity. Our Pirate Ship had spent fourteen months in a bubble. Now we'd have to expand to include them, and our lives would forever be intertwined in some way.

Best of all, there were so many Palin daughters! I'm a girl's girl, and have always felt like everybody's sister or everybody's girl next door. And suddenly, there were lots of new young women and little girls for me to make friends with, play with, laugh with. I could take them under my wing, look after them, the way I love looking after my little sister, Bridget. I could show them the ropes. Political rallies and stages and conventions had defined my childhood. (Even in utero: My mother was pregnant with me at the Republican convention in 1984.) Mostly I was excited to share with the Palin girls that wild, we're-in-this-together feeling of a big campaign.

Just minutes later, we were onstage—all of us, both families, showing the world what we looked like. It was impossible to guess how the world would react.

YOU KNOW HOW BEYONCÉ HAS HER ALTER PERSONA, Sasha Fierce? Well, I have one too. After the election, a blogger referred to me as Meggie Mac. And that is what I now call her. For me, she's the person who comes out on any stage, and talks in interviews. She is lively and polite, energetic and cheerful, and always tries to be great company. When I'm overwhelmed, Meggie Mac is there for me in clutch moments. It's hard to explain, but comforting to know I can tap into her. I can turn her on, become Meggie Mac, most of the time. And on that day, I thanked God that I could.

I don't have illusions about what my real job was on the campaign. I can talk about the blog and my moderate Republican fanbase until I'm blue in the face, but basically, all my job ever was, or would be— even if I became a First Daughter—was to stand up straight (chin up, core tight, it all helps with camera angles), keep a smile on my face, look admiringly at my father, and clap at the appropriate times.

Being a political prop isn't easy and it can mess with your mind. There are cameras on you, all the time. The entire traveling press corps stands right in front of you, staring and gawking and judging. You can't scratch your face or rub your nose. You can't yawn in boredom, or sit down when your feet start swelling.

The hardest part for me is seeing how reporters react. They show everything on their faces—much more than they know. Sometimes they don't bother trying to hide it, as though they stopped seeing you and your family as human beings, or even sentient creatures. After following us around for days, weeks, months, years . . . maybe they stop caring. The funny thing is that they don't seem to understand that they can become our entertainment as much as we become theirs.

From the stage, I could see everything that went on—*hellooo, you are sitting directly in front of me.* The press corps was often assembled on risers or on seats, and quite visible, but they acted as if we never saw them. They would gab on their cell phones and text in front of me. When they were bored, they would do yoga stretches, forward bends, or pick the goo out of their eyes. When they were actually listening, they would shake their heads and roll their eyes at something my father was saying. Unlike the audience members, who sat with open faces and seemed to have open minds, the traveling press corps seemed closed up, not interested, and 100 percent Team Obama, which they made very little effort to conceal.

Sometimes it ruined my Meggie Mac concentration if I started to think about how shut down they were, and how we couldn't reach them, how so many of them had already made up their minds that all Republicans are uncool or stupid or elitist or racist or whatever. We were like an ugly traveling circus to them, and a circus they'd seen too much of. They thought we were close-minded.

They seemed the most close-minded of all.

After the election was over, I saw a picture on Facebook of a campaign reporter's laptop screen as it faced out at a sea of stadium seats at a political convention. On the screen of the laptop, in giant letters, were the words "FUCK POLITICS."

This was meant to be funny, obviously, and drown us all in irony. I'm sure it can be awful to hear the same speeches over and over, hundreds of times. But isn't this journalist complaining about having front row seats to history? The more I thought about this picture, the more it bothered me. And sadly, it played into my own fears and insecurities about the media. It pretty much summed up what I already believed the traveling press corps was writing anyway: "Fuck politics!" oh yeah, and "Fuck Republicans!" because we've got Obama now, haven't you heard? *He's going to fix every problem this country has ever had!*

Of course, this made me want to shout and yell and scream. I know that a life in politics requires thick skin, or at least the ability to act as though you are impervious, or insensitive, or simply floating above the fray. But that wouldn't be me.

I did have a few tricks, though, for keeping myself collected onstage. I found if I started focusing on one particular reporter—watching him or her intently, and trying to notice every single thing about him or her—I could stay engaged and alert.

This mental exercise probably sounds boring, but I had ways of making it fascinating. For instance, if there were two reporters who had a thing for each other, and were always flirting, I would focus on them. Usually they made lots of intriguing attempts to cover up the fact that they were attracted to each other, but at the same time, it would be

almost impossible for them to be near each other at a rally or anywhere else, without flirting as though they were sitting in a bar.

I guess it's natural that I should enjoy turning the tables on people
who spend all their time studying my dad and mom and the rest of
our family, trying to learn our secrets so they can expose them. And
it's funny that reporters never seemed aware that we paid attention to
their behavior—or realized that, as much as gossip from inside the
campaign became known to the media, the gossip from the back of
the plane made its way to us.

The romantic antics of one female reporter kept me entertained for
months, as I followed the dramatic twists and turns of her flirting, over-
drinking, and crazy-sex. If I hadn't disliked her work so much, I might
have felt sorry for her.

It was witnessing behavior like that, not just between members of
the press corps, but inside our campaign as well—moments when I
saw people trying to cover up, or hide, or out-and-out lie—that helped
me create one of my mottos in life: *There are no secrets.* Even though it
is sometimes the most difficult thing in life, I always try to be up-
front and own my shit. If I'm up to something, I talk about it. If I do
something stupid or bad, I admit it. *There are no secrets.* Because one
way or another, all things are revealed. I believe that.

BUT I WANT TO GET BACK TO SARAH PALIN, AND THAT
day when I went onstage and stood clapping as my dad announced
that he couldn't wait to "introduce her to Washington, DC." As much
as I was excited by the news of the announcement, and that she was a
woman, I felt shaken and troubled. A wave of worry swept over me
and I remember thinking, I don't know anything about this woman
and neither does the rest of the country.

What are her politics really like? *Is she ready for this?* What went
through my head that night, and probably went through yours, were
questions and more questions. To be honest, her family didn't seem

ready for what was about to hit them. The original cast from *Saturday Night Live* (where I once worked) was called "The Not Ready for Prime Time Players." That's what the Palins looked like: not ready for prime time. They were so unprepared, in fact, that they were eerily calm, as though oblivious about what would come—the intrusions, distortions, and heat of the spotlight. But, I thought, maybe that's a good thing. The country was clearly ready for something different and organic and original. Sarah and her family were nothing if not that.

Was she truly a maverick like my dad? I knew virtually nothing about her, and the more I thought about all the other people who'd been passed over, particularly Joe Lieberman, an icy slap of panic hit me. Who is this person we've put so much of our trust in? And please, God, *don't let her have any horrible skeletons in her closet.*

Once the speech was done, and the world had its chance to meet Sarah Palin for the first time, my job was to work the rope line and pose for lots of photographs. This is basically an animated, vocalized version of my onstage role as cardboard political prop. That day, in my Meggie Mac mode, I talked about how excited I was about my father's campaign and his running mate, and kept my panic to myself.

After the rope line, we went upstairs—members of both families—for a *People* magazine shoot that I hadn't known about. I was a living mess, and feeling worse every second, and barely able to look at my mother. The photographer herded us together, frantically trying to make visual sense of us, but it was a daunting task.

Later, my mother and I met, hoping to clear the air. We discussed a number of things that troubled both of us—the mysterious selection process, as well as the selection of Sarah herself. I told my mother how blindsided I felt. It was an uncomfortable conversation and, in many ways, opened up more uncomfortable subjects. Over the past fourteen months, I had felt pretty knowledgeable about the inner workings of the campaign. Suddenly I realized that I was pretty naïve and I had been kept in the dark about many things.

Sarah Palin had been chosen in secret, apparently by the campaign advisers Steve Schmidt, Charlie Black, Mark Salter, and Rick Davis. She had been vetted quickly and when she passed, she had been invited to Sedona, where my family has a ranch—as had all the other potential running mates—to meet my mom and dad.

After our talk, I felt better about a few things. Namely, I stopped blaming my parents for keeping me in the dark about a decision that was so important, not just to the campaign but to my family personally. I realized it had been truly a collective campaign decision—made by my father and advisers and professionals whom he trusted and liked. I was an outsider, even on my father's campaign. In some ways, it had been my own choosing. My parents were probably smart to keep me out of the loop. If they had told me about Sarah Palin earlier, I would have discussed it with Shannon and Heather. Like I said, *there are no secrets.* So don't tell me one.

As all of these revelations were sinking in, I began to feel scared in a way that I had never been before—and felt different about the outcome of the election. Before, I had always felt certain that my dad would get the nomination and win. I had never doubted it. But now I was worried. How the Palin selection process and announcement had been handled seemed to highlight things that were innately wrong with our campaign and with the tactics of Steve Schmidt. It was a risky move—one of those things that can wind up being genius or the stupidest decision of all time. More than anything, it seemed like gambling.

Like my father, I have always been more of a craps girl than a strategic poker player. Actually, roulette is my favorite game. Screw it, I thought. Let's spin the wheel and see where the ball winds up.

4

THE BIRTH OF BLOGETTE

WHEN I FIRST JOINED THE CAMPAIGN, IT WAS HARD TO GET INTO THE PACE—OR FIGURE OUT WHAT MY ROLE WOULD BE. I WANTED TO find a way to fit in, stay out of trouble, and contribute something of value. The campaign was a small band in those days, a tight group. My real job as a daughter-of was mostly cosmetic and decorative. I was supposed to stand straight, wave, smile, and look nice, but not *too* nice. (No skin, no *bling!*) But I wanted to contribute more.

I'm sure there was some eye-rolling at campaign headquarters when word got out that I wanted to write a blog. As anybody who's interned or worked in their mom's or dad's office knows, you can get pegged as a raging brat really fast. The smell of entitlement oozes from your skin and follows you around like a cloud, no matter what you do.

But as serendipity would have it, Rick Davis was running the campaign in those days. Rick is charming—a handsome older-guy type with wire-rim glasses and old-school suits and ties. He always picked up the phone when I called, and laughed at my jokes. He believed in me or, at least, had the good manners to act like it. He cut me some slack, the way my dad always did. And I needed it.

Let's face it. As far as politics went, I was hardly a super-skilled professional. I had just graduated from Columbia with a degree in art history, an academic discipline that I love and was serious about in college. I had no experience in fieldwork or political strategy. Aside from my shit detector and gut, which, thank God, were often on target, I knew very little about campaigning.

But I do have a sixth sense about the Internet, and an ability to combine large amounts of information and create a focused, toned-down segment. I had worked as a paid summer intern for *Newsweek* magazine and followed a number of blogs. This, combined with the fact that I'm a nonstop extrovert, a people person who loves mingling and gabbing and getting out in the world, a blog that chronicled my days on the campaign—and showed the silliness and madness, as well as the seriousness—seemed like a perfect idea. Sheer genius! Or so I thought.

My mother loved the idea, became my biggest supporter, and pushed pretty hard for the campaign to let me do it. Once I had agreed to pay for all the costs of the blog, including staff and travel, how could they turn me down? Still, it took convincing and a fair amount of drama and, of course, lawyers had to get involved.

But I am stubborn, and always have been—and I was determined to make it happen and used voter demographics to argue my case. The audience that I would reach with a blog, or hoped to, was one that all the collected eggheads of my father's campaign—the strategists and polling experts—had the most trouble with: young moderates and independents. The Republican National Committee had raised and spent millions of dollars on market research, and come up with zillions of ideas about using the Internet, but we had little presence there.

Republicans "got" radio. Conservatives were heard, loud and clear, on those airwaves. But aside from viral lies and mudslinging, like the Swift Boat Campaign against John Kerry, which was a really shameful moment in political history, the party just didn't get the digital scene. What year was this? 2007. And the presidential campaign was poised to be groundbreaking in terms of communication tactics and media. Digital was definitely the place to be. For a political candidate, the blogosphere was exciting, persuasive, and reached voters instantly. Best of all, aside from production costs, it was free. There was Facebook, MySpace, and a day didn't go by without YouTube. The old world of print journalism was making a crash landing.

And yet, the Republican Party was stuck in the tar pits, waiting (yet again) for the country to time travel back to the beloved Reagan era, as if wishing could make it so. (The irony is that the Reagan administration was so forward-thinking and creative when it came to media.) But these days, the unwillingness of the Republican Party to enter the real world stunned me.

Young people found their news on Internet sites and blogs—and were comfortable with outlets like *The Daily Show* and *The Colbert Report,* that combined frivolity, even occasional vulgarity, with straight reporting and commentary. But so far, I couldn't see what was being offered online that might help my dad's race. Most of the news sites were left-leaning and made little effort to even conceal it. Politico, which was launched in January 2007, was smart and not angry—it felt like real reporting without a noticeable political bent, which made it the exception—but it wasn't exactly a laugh riot.

It's not that young people can't be serious. But they are accustomed to being entertained—and are drawn to reality shows and, at least, a feeling of realness that a good blog creates. My idea was to produce a daily record of campaign highlights as seen through my eyes and, more than anything, update the image of Republicans. If we were going to attract a younger following, we really had to start there.

In politics, passion counts for a lot. The side with the most juice and spirit, and the loudest voices, gets heard the most. This is why, politically, the Republican Party is drifting toward the interests of the Christian Right, who are organized and very passionate. Moderates, by comparison, come off as compliant and easygoing and kind of weak-spirited. It's like they have nothing except their equanimity to organize themselves around.

So if you are young and moderate, like me and tens of millions of other voters, you are part of the great misunderstood—and missed—voting bloc. But we count for as much as one-third of the electorate.

Young people are passionate, that's for sure. But they aren't scared and filled with hate. They are excited by change, new ideas, and fresh starts. It must be a law of nature. The young are meant to challenge the status quo and question conventions. Our job is to critique the progress made by the previous generation and push back with new ideas.

But lately, in the Republican Party, anybody with a new idea is labeled "progressive," that dirty word, or just ignored. I can't think of a greater turn-off. Why would a vibrant young person, full of energy and passion and lots of creativity, be interested in the Republican Party if new ideas and fresh starts aren't welcome? This might explain why the vast majority of the under-thirty vote aren't registered Republicans.

When I joined the campaign, I wasn't even one.

5

ELEPHANTS IN THE BATHROOM

M Y PERIOD OF TOTAL ESTRANGEMENT FROM THE REPUBLICAN PARTY BEGAN WHEN I WAS FIFTEEN. I'M SURE THAT I DIDN'T UNDER- stand the concept of principles at that age, or what the political parties stood for. I had grown up in an insular world where conservative thought was accepted, and its basic tenets weren't challenged, so I didn't have too many opportunities to think about them much.

That's how it works, usually. If things are handed to you easily, even if they are ideas and beliefs, you take them for granted and don't bother evaluating them. That's how it was for me, anyway, as a little girl. My mom used to dress me up in red-white-and-blue outfits and give me a flag to wave at rallies. I assumed that everybody was a Republican, and that everybody collected as many elephants and as much elephant iconography as my parents did. We had them all over our house in Phoenix—elephant sculptures, paintings, picture frames, and wall hangings. We even had an elephant bathroom that had elephant wallpaper with small bronze and silver elephants in it. I had my own elephant collection too.

Really, until my dad ran for president the first time, in 2000, I had a very idyllic, all-American, and sheltered childhood—devoid of much awareness about my father's fame or his job or even politics. My mom ran the house and our lives, pretty much, cooking our dinner most nights and gathering us around the table, where we were each asked to describe "the high" and "the low" of our day. Mom has always been the go-to person in our lives, the parent who solved our problems and dispensed practical advice and knowledge. She can tell you how a plane flies, how a car is put together, and how to unstop a plugged toilet or balance a checkbook.

Our house was always busy, a little messy, and crazy noisy. The louder and noisier it is, the more Mom loves it, especially if it's filled with kids and animals. Over the years, we've had five fish tanks, packs of dogs and cats, and a beloved parade of pet hamsters, bunnies, turtles, and even a ferret named Daisy.

My dad called every day from his office in DC, but he rarely brought up his work, or political matters. We talked about my stuff, how school was and whether I was fighting with Jack and Jimmy, my younger brothers, whom I liked to boss around. Dad made me laugh—he always does—telling me stupid jokes. On weekends, he flew home and liked to relax by watching football or grilling, which he's passionate about. He'd drive us all up to Sedona, where our family ranch is, and listened to sports on the radio the whole time, even when the radio station started to fade away and get scratchy as we drove farther from the city.

When I think of how much hiking I did as a kid, it makes me laugh. Dad loves to hike—and build dams in the creek with piles of rock. And every year, no matter how hot it is, he and my brothers go camping in the Grand Canyon and sleep in smelly tents.

He still doesn't "feel" famous to me, he feels like my dorky dad who came to tea parties in my bedroom and let me put bows and clips in his hair when I was little. To me, he's the dad who snores so loud it wakes up the dogs, the dad who makes the most disgusting fried eggs with tons of grease, and makes the best campfires ever.

When I think of him, I think of the Father's Day when my kindergarten class went on a father-daughter picnic out in the Arizona mountains, and all of the girls gave their fathers tie-dye T-shirts that we'd made for them as gifts. All the other dads stood around in their regular clothes, their polo shirts and whatnot, smiling and holding their tie-dye shirts in their hands. But my dad immediately tugged off his shirt in front of everyone and put the tie-dye shirt on. All the teachers began clapping and it started a trend with the other dads, who put on their tie-dye shirts too. I remember being so embarrassed while it was happening, because my dad is so hairy—he has a ton of white and gray chest hair—and then he kissed me on the cheek and said, "Anything you made I will love forever."

That's how I think of my dad. A trendsetter, doing things before everyone else, taking risks and loving everything about me. The tie-dye shirt, that's how I see him. I wasn't much older when he taught me how to hook a worm and fish in the creek at Sedona, and gladly took me to see *The Little Mermaid,* the Disney movie, seven times. When we played in the swimming pool in Phoenix, he would throw me in, over and over again, and make me scream with laughter.

I was just fifteen when he ran for president for the first time, and things changed quickly. I remember being shocked when I heard that he was parodied on *Saturday Night Live.* Wow, I thought, he must really be known if *SNL* is parodying him!

For lots of reasons, I was really excited that he was running. I'm sure most girls love feeling proud of their dads. But I have always felt a particularly deep bond with mine, a sense that we almost share the same soul. He gets me and always has.

My memories of watching him campaign in New Hampshire in 2000 are really vivid. I hadn't spent much time in snowy New England, and hadn't been exposed to its gorgeous, almost storybook setting. It is hard for me to put it into words, but New England almost doesn't seem real to me. And my memories of New Hampshire are so strong, like a beautiful movie that I can step into.

For those who have trouble keeping the election process straight in their heads, New Hampshire follows the Iowa caucus by a few days, so it is one of the most important primaries of the campaign and has the potential to shift national preferences, sometimes dramatically. You can start out an underdog, but if you win New Hampshire, you are suddenly a frontrunner. You win New Hampshire and you have momentum, and promise. A domino effect kicks in. You win New Hampshire and the campaign donations start flooding in too.

My dad was an underdog in the race in 2000. George W. Bush had come away the victor of the Iowa caucus, had a much bigger campaign war chest, and was leading in the polls with 64 percent of the predicted vote. Dad had only 15 percent. But he is never one to give up. He loves New Hampshire, particularly for the way politics gets done there—town hall by town hall.

The best thing in the world for me was seeing him conduct a town hall. I watched in total amazement, aware immediately that he loved every second of it—the contact with people, the setting, and the bizarre and surprising range of questions. He listened, looked people in the eye, and answered their questions in the same way that he answered all the life questions I asked him when I was growing up. He was comfortable and real, and so strong.

I had never seen anything like it—democracy in its truest form, unclouded—and I remember feeling so proud of my dad. People still referred to him as the "grand master of the town hall" and sometimes "the governor of New Hampshire." His town halls were jam-packed with people, wherever we went. The experience was so beautiful and emotional. Politics was personal, I saw that so powerfully. At fifteen, maybe I didn't really understand all the ideals. But I understood the feelings.

Veterans talked about their military service, elderly people confessed they couldn't afford their prescriptions, mothers brought their disabled children—and everything else in between. It made me feel giddy and sad, all at once, a roller coaster of feelings. I remember somebody asking my dad how he felt about "hemp" and, not knowing that this was a question about smoking it, he answered that it was great for "making rope." We had a good laugh about it for years.

Our mood was high, and we were so hopeful. When he won in New Hampshire that year—a stunning upset of nineteen points against George W. Bush—it was the biggest upset of the political year. Everything was focused on South Carolina, the next primary, just two and a half weeks later. Bush had a fifty-point lead there, but he was losing ground. After New Hampshire, my father was closing in.

This is where things become ugly and sad. What happened in South Carolina in 2000 is what caused me to reconsider everything, and draw away from politics. My father lost in South Carolina, but he didn't lose fair and square. He lost as a result of one of the dirtiest political tricks ever played. A hate campaign was waged against him and our family—a campaign that spread lies and fear.

E-mails went around, and became viral, saying that my dad had "sired children out of wedlock." There was mention of a "Negro child." Pamphlets—thousands of them—were stuck under car windshields showing a photograph of all of us, my mom and dad; me; my brothers, Jack and Jimmy; and my sweet sister, Bridget, who was adopted by my parents from a Bangladesh orphanage when she was a baby. The pamphlets led people to believe that Bridget was the "Negro child" my father had sired out of wedlock.

Something called "push polls" were conducted. Republican voters were called at home and informed that my father was mentally unstable from his years in prison as a POW or a Manchurian candidate secretly planning to spread communism. There were mentions of the "Negro child" during the push polls, and my mother, who had struggled with a prescription drug addiction after back surgery six years before—and had talked publicly about it—was smeared as a drug addict.

It was sick, disgusting—and everything it will go down in history for being. And it was so dirty and secret that it became impossible to trace who was responsible, directly or indirectly, except to know the man who won that primary: George W. Bush.

For my family, it was devastating. My whole world, the people whom I loved most, my parents, and brothers, and baby sister, were suddenly at the center of ugliness and unwanted attention. To lose a race is hard enough. But to lose unfairly is brutal and haunting. I blocked out the pain, and tried to forget, but at the same time, it stayed with me—the way feelings do when you try to ignore them. Someday I'd want to know what happened, I figured, but not yet.

Three or four years later, when I was in college, I came across an article in *Vanity Fair* that went into explicit detail about the South Carolina primary, and I remember feeling really uncomfortable reading it. I wanted to know the details, but at the same time, I didn't. My mom had explained a few things—but not too much.

She had been waiting until we asked questions, and were old enough to understand, except I don't think there is a way to understand.

People in politics, and those of us raised in political families, are told not to take politics personally. But, of course, we do. We must. Otherwise the world of politics will become even more dehumanizing and impersonal. If we don't take politics personally, we aren't honoring what it means to be human—and risk winding up as cruel and unfeeling, as inhuman, as the ones who spread lies and win unfairly.

The trick, I think, is to remain human and just forgive.

My father moved on—that's how he is, he moves forward, doesn't look back, doesn't get burdened by hate or the wrong actions of others. He leaves things for history to judge. But for my mom, and the rest of us who love him so much, it was impossible. Eventually, when I was in college, I asked my mother about South Carolina. And I guess my brothers, Jack and Jimmy, eventually did too.

But my little sister, Bridget, the youngest in our family, didn't know anything about it until she was sixteen years old and, just for kicks, she happened to google her own name and found herself linked, in almost every item, to the South Carolina primary of 2000.

She called me immediately, extremely upset, crying, and—not understanding what had happened—she feared that somehow she, and the color of her beautiful skin, had affected the outcome of that election, and caused our father to lose the race. It was heartbreaking, so heartbreaking.

I told her a few things that I knew, mostly that it was sick, and screwed-up people did things like that. I told her that I believed in karma—and that what goes around comes around, and those events will live with President Bush and Karl Rove, his creepy campaign "mastermind," and with the individuals from the Christian Coalition who had helped to orchestrate it and did the push polls.

I told her that I loved her and that it was our job to make sure that things like this didn't happen in politics again, because it was wrong and terrible for our country.

"Does President Bush hate me?" she asked.

This was the saddest of all.

"No," I said. "He can't hate you. He doesn't even know you."

"Why did he do it?"

"He just wanted to win."

We've all moved on now, my whole family, including Bridget. My father set the tone and we followed. He has taught us about looking forward, forgiving and moving on. But when I was nineteen and registering to vote in a presidential election for the first time in 2004, it wasn't possible for me to vote for a man who had been responsible, directly or indirectly, for causing so much sadness and pain in my family and for debasing the democratic process with dirty tactics and smears. He had never apologized or even distanced himself from the wrongful actions of his followers.

At nineteen, politics was only personal to me and not distinguishable from my feelings about my family. So it was out of anger, and sadness, really, that I registered as independent and voted for John Kerry. I didn't switch my party affiliation and officially become a Republican until June 2008, after nearly a year on the road with my father's campaign.

Hard-core conservatives focus on this fact now, a way to dismiss me as not conservative enough, an untrustworthy "progressive," a Manchurian daughter, a RINO or a "Republican in Name Only." But I think if they walked a mile in my shoes—something my dad always taught me to do before sitting down to judge another person—they'd understand.

6

SHANNON AND HEATHER

M Y BROTHERS AND SISTER AND I WERE TOO YOUNG AT THE TIME OF THE 2000 PRESIDENTIAL RACE TO BE ALLOWED ON THE ROAD. WE were flown in for big moments, like town halls in New Hampshire and a few primary election nights. But my parents felt that the day-to-day work of a national political campaign was not a place for kids. It was a stressful environment, the air is charged with complicated emotions—ones that aren't easy for kids to process.

But back at our house in Phoenix, my parents had stacks of photo albums from the race. In high school, I would sometimes sit for hours and look at them. I saw the happy faces in the crowd, the streamers of the rallies and parties, the sea of people at the convention. I wondered, what was it *really* like? What else went on?

These photo albums became the inspiration for my blog, McCain-Blogette. Along with writing, I wanted a photo-driven record of day-to-day events too—something that felt spontaneous, a bit gritty, and maybe too real.

★

FOR THE FIRST FOUR MONTHS THAT I WAS ON THE CAM-paign, I worked on the design of the blog and lined up a team to help me. Of course, there were flubs and mini-dramas of all kinds. Before I was given final approval, Rick Davis and others told me that I had to hire somebody with experience and political credentials to oversee content. I didn't like the "oversee" part of that. And I was pretty skepti-cal when campaign staff said they'd found such a person, a guy named Rob Kubasko. But Rob turned out to be a tall, adorable computer-geek type and we got along immediately, and in the end, became very close friends. Without him, the blog would never have worked.

Rob is a total font of political know-how, both lore and statistics, exactly the kind of internal database that I was lacking. In school, and generally in life, I had stayed pretty far away from politics and politi-cal history, a massive hole in my education that so many people in my dad's professional life seemed to find surprising. I had enrolled in pre-cisely one political science course in college and on the first day, the McCain-Feingold bill was discussed at length. It made me so uncom-fortable to be discussing the campaign reform legislation that my dad cared so passionately about, I quickly dropped the class.

Children of doctors and lawyers aren't expected to know the intri-cate details of surgery or habeas corpus. But people are often shocked to discover that I didn't spend my youth following bills in Congress or falling asleep at night counting all the White House chiefs of staff in chronological order in my head. When you grow up in political Wash-ington, DC—which I didn't—maybe all this is second nature to you, kind of like growing up in LA and knowing the names of all the hot new rock bands because they are playing at the clubs down the street.

In Arizona, I grew up riding horses, fishing with my dad, wrestling with my brothers, and going to Dunkin' Donuts every Friday before school with my mom and siblings. I'm happy that's how it was. My parents did not want us to be Washington kids with Washington know-how.

But being plunged into the bizarre world of political junkies and campaign diehards was jarring at the beginning. People talked non-stop about issues, strategy, and ideas, which was stimulating and exciting. But physically, the campaign trail was hard duty—and the schedule was hysterically busy. It was like transient prison life, where the only things I was in control of, for the most part, were my clothes, my hair, and the blog. Even in the early, supposedly sleepy days before the primaries, the pace was go-go-go and we were flying and busing around nonstop.

Shannon Bae and Heather Brand were with me every step of the way. We were inseparable, and I refused to get on a bus or plane, or go to an event, if they couldn't be included too. They weren't just my co-horts, fellow Blogettes, or roommates. They were like my big sisters, my bodyguards—and a safety net. God knows I needed them.

The three of us were always trudging from one campaign event to the next, while, from a distance, either in Phoenix or at headquarters in DC, Rob guided the overall program and formatted pictures. I joked that he was Charlie to our angels because we were always getting into jams or being denied access—the Secret Service agents never seemed to know who I was—but Rob's voice on the phone would ground us and focus us.

Shannon, who made the video segments for the blog, is a curvy Korean-American with a love of plunging necklines, tattoos, and piercings. Heather was our beautiful blog photographer and a kind woman with a sweet temperament. She and I had met during my freshman year at Columbia University when she came to take a photograph of me when I needed one, and we've been friends ever since. Later, she introduced me to Shannon, whom she had met while working on the TV show *K Street*.

I idolize Shannon and Heather for many reasons. One of Heather's most admirable qualities is how, unlike me, she keeps her life impressively drama-free. If only I could pull that off—to be the sort of person who goes through life with effortless calm and grace and even temper, never making waves or having to apologize. But that's just not me. As my mom used to say, "If only I'd known I was giving birth to John McCain in a dress."

Heather is one person whom nobody ever had a problem with on the campaign, or anywhere else. She is also the only person I would trust to take pictures of my family in some emotionally raw and vulnerable situations, which were produced nonstop in the roller-coaster days of that year. We all trust Heather, and love her. And her talent with the camera is amazing and the way she expresses herself best.

If Heather is an earthy goddess, I guess that Shannon is a temptress—a sultry provocateur with a video camera. She is honest, open-minded, and fair. Without seeming to try, Shannon is admired and desired too, particularly by men. Although women are drawn to her infectious personality, Shannon draws guys to her like nobody I've ever seen. On the campaign, the dorkiest Republican volunteers would be stumbling behind her, swooning and going gaga.

"Everyone falls in love with Shannon," I'd say, and I had to say it a lot. I should have made a sign and hung it around my neck.

Her secret is easy to understand but hard to duplicate. Shannon knows who she is, and is so secure in herself, and who she is as a person—inside and out—that it is infectious. More than almost anyone else in my life, she has helped me grow as a person and remain true to myself. I am so grateful for my friendship with both Shannon and Heather. I am not sure I could have survived the election without them.

FOR OUR VERY FIRST LIVE POSTING, IN OCTOBER 2007, we went to an event at the Hotel Valley Ho, one of my all-time favorite hotels in Phoenix, where my dad had spoken to a group of young professionals. Trying to keep things light and funny, I hammed it up in a few photos, one with my dad and another with my mom, who had hurt her knee and was on crutches, but was smiling nonetheless and wearing a beautiful black cocktail dress.

Within a few hours, the annihilating criticism started. It was brutal, kind of like baptism by acid. A Washington, DC–based gossip blog called Wonkette was the first to have a go. The screaming headline said it all: "JOHN MCCAIN'S OTHER DAUGHTER HAS A LAME BLOG!!!"

Here's the rest:

Hey everybody, John McCain's daughter "Meghan" has a blog all about, uh, "young professionals" and their alleged main activity, which is going to a John McCain campaign event in Phoenix, called the "Valley Ho." The blog is only a few days old, but it can already make people cringe like a blog that's been around for years! Oh and Cindy McCain is on crutches. She probably hurt herself breaking into a pharmacy.

Horrified, I scrolled down to look at the readers' comments, hoping people would have written in to defend my mom or me. But their remarks were even worse, a dark pit of meanness, mostly about me. Readers had said things like: "She makes the girls from the Bada Bing club look fresh," referring to the strippers on *The Sopranos*. Yeah, real nice stuff.

I was a total mess—who wouldn't be?—and cried for hours. My mother was so comforting, and told me everything a mother tells you in situations like that, so soothing and never focusing on the stuff said about her. But I was crushed. Who were these people and how could they hate me so quickly? I felt confused, and angry. We'd been live for less than twenty-four hours and I was already a bada bing girl and my blog was lame.

As much of an Internet junkie as I was, I had never read anything like it—and until then, hadn't realized what an ugly and raw place the blogosphere can be. Every day, we posted new things and every day, there were new comments from readers. People wrote to rant and criticize and also to send thanks and encouragement. Some were sweet, some were sad, and some were scary and had to be reported to the FBI.

Sometimes I think people write things on blogs, websites, and comment boards just to vent and let it out—not expecting anyone to actually read it. But I did. Eventually Rob told me to stop, and produced an edited version of the comments for me to see. I peeked anyway.

Criticism, I learned, had a way of motivating me. I kept plugging on—and had a strong vision for the blog—determined to do something new, and go behind the scenes, to show things that weren't going to be seen otherwise. Some of it was playful and meant to be a little naughty. I wanted it to have an unscripted quality, and be taken from our daily life—food platters, homemade signs, the bus bathroom, people sleeping in strange places, adviser Mark McKinnon's "lucky" hat, a spontaneous visit to Walmart.

But internal complaints poured in. There were many, many problems with campaign staffers not wanting their picture taken, or just unhappy with things we posted on the blog. It was too silly, too sarcastic, too everything. More than anyone, the blog seemed to irritate Steve Schmidt, who took over as campaign manager during primary season. As a political consultant, Steve had organized the confirmation hearings of John Roberts and Samuel Alito to the Supreme Court and run Arnold Schwarzenegger's reelection campaign for governor of California. But he seemed like a latecomer to me, and I resented him for simply not being Rick Davis, whom I adored. My dad certainly had faith in Steve on the big things, and big decisions. Months later, Steve made a strong case for anointing Sarah Palin as the running mate and my father listened to him. But my own interactions with Steve were complicated.

He was always turning me down, denying me access, or just plain ignoring me. I was an irritating insect to him, and one that he wished would fly away—or drop dead. Whatever I thought I was bringing to the campaign, in terms of attitude, energy, creativity, and young followers, seemed beside the point to him. As the campaign progressed and the stakes got higher, and the environment became tense, Shannon and Heather and I were increasingly not allowed to go places, or to take pictures.

I am one of the most stubborn individuals I know, but eventually I had to concede that Steve Schmidt was even more stubborn.

He's also about three times my size. A tall man with a wide chest and big paunch, a shiny cue-ball head, and a Bluetooth glued to his ear, Steve exudes a completely different vibe from the calm, gentlemanly Rick Davis, who had green-lighted my blog in the beginning. Steve is the polar opposite of Rick, in fact—and seems to enjoy being tough, terse, and intimidating to almost everyone. He's a drill sergeant. I'm five foot one and sometimes when I stood next to him, I felt like Dorothy facing down the giant bald head of the Wizard of Oz—at least, before she realizes he's just the threatened old man behind the curtain.

I'll confess, I had some seriously juvenile moments with Blogette, and aggravating Steve Schmidt was exhilarating at times. We weren't above easy little revenges. Bucking against his tyrannical control was fun—and Shannon and Heather and I reveled in our misdeeds.

We put up crappy pictures of people and journalists we didn't like on the site, knowing how pissed off they'd be. One time Mark Salter, who is my dad's alter ego and speechwriter, and coauthor of his books, fell asleep on the campaign plane and we put plastic cockroaches and plastic bugs all over his arms and shoulders and took pictures of him. If you have ever met Mark you know how seriously he can take himself—and you would know how *not down* he'd be with being photographed covered in plastic bugs, which is probably why it became such a popular picture that generated lots of feedback and comments. And it's probably why his sister found it so funny.

Looking back on our antics, and our little power plays with the blog, they were pretty innocuous. And our successes were small ones too. At the time, I was thrilled those first months as my audience rose to one thousand hits per day, and later stunned when it rose to ten thousand—and the next year, as high as eighty thousand in a day. I had never really generated much attention in my life, except for the love and support and applause my parents always gave me. So to me, this was the big time. Compared to a healthy website or blog today, our following was meager. And compared to the creative stuff that Hillary Clinton and Barack Obama's web teams were up to, my efforts seem amateurish and small-time.

I had bigger dreams for the blog—and began to see ways, almost immediately, that we could draw more hits—but I didn't have the money to do much PR or to update throughout the day, which I had learned is how you keep people following you. In the end, I'm not sure Blogette lived up to my dreams for it, but I tried, and kept trying. I cared so much.

Hindsight is 20/20, the old expression goes, but I do wonder how much more we could have done, and how many more young voters we could have reached, if our Internet operations had been more effective across the board. The conventional wisdom at the time, especially within the Republican establishment, was that chasing young voters too diligently was a waste of time and money. Young voters were supposed to be a lousy bet, fickle and almost impossible to get into the voting booth. They might be passionate during rallies, but come election day, they would have moved on to a new interest, another candidate—or have bought a new iPod and forgotten about the election completely.

The Democrats hadn't given up on the young—or given up trying creative new ways to excite them, or use the Internet. Hillary Clinton and Barack Obama were waging a crazy battle for attention on the web with e-mail campaigns and hilarious video send-ups, using humor and irreverence. Their campaigns both found a tone and style online that worked with the young, and kept them engaged.

The rewards of this aren't even worth debating. By the time primary season was over, and Hillary had conceded, the Obama campaign had employed innovative young techno-geeks to develop a state-of-the-art web operation and strategy that helped them win two-thirds of the youth vote in the general election while selling millions and millions of T-shirts and posters at the same time. My generation proved that it can be relied upon to contribute, to volunteer, and to vote.

My hope is that in 2012, the young are given more of a choice—and fought over even harder—and that the Republican Party will be up to the challenge.

7

HEARTLAND HEADACHES

Y DAD IS INCREDIBLY SUPERSTITIOUS. MY WHOLE FAMILY IS, PROBABLY BECAUSE OF HIM. HIS SUPERSTITIOUSNESS IS INFECTIOUS, and if you spend time around him, you wind up collecting good luck charms and participating in lots of good luck rituals. That's why, right after Iowa, where my dad trailed behind Mike Huckabee and Mitt Romney, somebody sent in a little statue of Saint Jude, the patron saint of lost causes, to campaign headquarters. He was supposed to bring us the juice.

I'd been on the road for half a year by then, posting on the blog every day for the last four months. It was brutal, a hamster wheel. The blog was like a wild animal that is always hungry, never satisfied. Every day it needs more. After two weeks straight of feeding it and scrambling around like a crazy person to make sure the blog was as good as it could be, I'd take four days off, usually a long weekend vegetating at home in Phoenix to unwind. Actually, it wasn't really enough time to relax, but you could do laundry, repack, and sleep in. Mostly I lived in my pajamas and UGG boots, ate takeout, and went to movies with my normal Arizona friends who weren't obsessed with the election.

Before long I was itching for the madness of the campaign again—for the laughs, the boring bus trips, the roller-coaster rides of emotion. Instead of becoming drained by the campaign process, or dispirited by our loss in Iowa, or that the campaign was running out of money again, I became more and more charged. I was so excited to be on the campaign, and so sure we'd win, at night I could barely sleep.

To me, we were never a lost cause. Even after Iowa. But to most everybody else, particularly the media, Mitt Romney was the man to watch.

Saint Jude was a little guy, about eight inches tall, the size of those little plastic Jesus figures that people put in the back windows of their cars. And wouldn't you know—he did have the juice. Once he arrived, we won and kept winning. He was given a place on Rick Davis's desk at headquarters and nobody was allowed to move him.

I LOVE THE IDEA OF THE HEARTLAND, AND LIKE TO think of myself as a heartland girl, but being in Iowa, before the primaries began, made me think twice about that. The state is so flat, so endlessly flat, and the air smells like farms and fertilizer. I'm sure rotting manure is a really good smell for some people, all that natural waste and decay. But to me, it just smells like manure.

Events were miles apart and the bus rides went on and on.

I'll tell you what did delight me in the flatlands of Iowa—the crazy hotels. They appear in the middle of nowhere, outrageous and imaginative, like mini Vegas attractions. I remember specifically a fabulous hotel in Des Moines that had a waterslide as a centerpiece. The floors leading to the hotel rooms are covered in Astroturf and each room has a fantastically tacky tropical theme—along the lines of *National Lampoon's Vacation*. I loved every single room I saw, and

Heather took tons of pictures. We still joke that my next project should be a coffee table book of the most creative hotels throughout the country.

You get to be a connoisseur of weird hotels on a campaign—and accustomed to things that would otherwise bug you or even repulse you in other phases of your life. For instance, after six months on the road, whenever Shannon and Heather and I checked into a cheap hotel where the campaign was staying, we just assumed that there would be pubic hair on the toilet seat, or on the side of the bathtub. We had a technique for dealing with it. We used a blow-dryer to blow the hairs off, if the electrical cord was long enough.

It became second nature to us. We almost stopped making a big deal out of it, and stopped hopping up and down and screaming because we were so grossed out. We just went into the bathroom, plugged in the blow-dryer, and went to work.

The worst hotel that I remember was in Iowa as well—a hotel so bleak, and so do-it-yourself, that my dad had to help us haul our big suitcases up two flights of stairs to our room. Out in the hallway, there was an ancient vending machine with cans of Coke that looked twenty years old. Our room was so terrible, there wasn't even a closet, just a bar on the wall where you could hang your clothes, but the hangers were soldered onto that bar, so nobody could steal them. The light-bulb in the bathroom was just that—a bare lightbulb and a chain. Who says politics is glamorous?

A couple hours after checking in, we found a box with a half-eaten pizza on the floor of the hallway outside our room—and this disgusted us completely. What jerk would leave old pizza on the floor? And why was it in front of our door? We invented a scenario in our heads, and then convinced ourselves it was true: The journalist in the room next to ours had dumped the old pizza there. What a slob! We couldn't believe it! In retribution, we put a plate of hard-boiled eggs outside his door, hoping he'd step on them as he took off on his daily run at dawn. And we were stumbling in hysteria the next morning when we saw that he had. Victory!

But upon climbing aboard the bus, my dad perked up when he saw us. "Hey, how'd you like the pizza I left you last night?"

I SHOULD PROBABLY EXPLAIN, FOR THOSE WHO DON'T know, that Iowa doesn't have a primary. There's a tradition of a "caucus" instead, something that dates back to the dark ages of 1972. It's a controversial and a completely different animal from a primary. Rather than going to the voting booth, as you would in a general election, and quietly voting by yourself, each county of Iowa elects delegates to cast a vote for all the eligible voters living in their district. It is much more time-consuming than a regular primary, to the point of being ridiculously inefficient.

The Iowa caucus for Republicans is historically very conservative, almost radically so. We all suspected that Romney would win. He and his sons had traveled to every county of Iowa in their damn camper—something they bragged about every chance they got. They hit Iowa hard, just as they should have. That was a smart strategy. But then Mike Huckabee, the former governor of Arkansas, swooped in with all his folksy mojo and beat him.

I have a lot of complaints about Mike Huckabee—he could be an entire chapter—but I'll give you the two main reasons why he is a Republican I could never vote for. Number one, he thinks being gay is immoral and perverted and equivalent to bestiality. Number two, he came up with a plan in 1992 to have all people who were HIV-positive sent to one area of the country by themselves, isolated from the general population like lepers in medieval times.

That kind of thinking is not just backward, it is dangerous. And I never, ever have been able to wrap my head around Mike Huckabee's appeal.

And the fact that Mike Huckabee eventually won in Iowa is, to me, just more evidence that our country's electoral college and primary system is outmoded. Particularly for Republicans, the process no longer is an adequate lens into the party as a whole. The states of Iowa and South Carolina, where primary trends begin, are specifically very conservative. And I have to worry that, down the road, in 2012 or 2016, with a split widening between moderates and hyperconservatives, that the party will be forced to go even more conservative than in the last election, because the system now favors a very conservative Republican nominee.

The drawbacks to this are enormous. The country does not seem to be riding a particularly conservative wave right now, and young people, especially, are not enamored of a hyperconservative agenda. After all, the country just elected the most liberal presidential candidate possible in the last election. The conservative pundits may scream that my dad isn't "conservative enough," but what other Republicans are electable? If you don't believe me, just give Mike Huckabee a try in the next election cycle and see a bloodbath ensue. A hyperconservative candidate has no chance of winning against President Obama. That is why the Republican party has to start being open to new people, new blood, and new ideas.

DON'T GET ME WRONG. WE SPENT LOTS OF TIME IN Iowa, even though it was a slog. But New Hampshire mattered in a different way. My dad was beloved there—partly due to his big win in 2000, and the stories about the South Carolina primary that followed. If Romney won in New Hampshire, we were cooked. It wasn't just my dad's strategy. It mattered to all the candidates, since historically a good number of individuals who win the presidency win in New Hampshire first.

So while Romney and the Five Brothers were appearing in every inch of Iowa, my dad spent more time in New Hampshire, and had more events there, which seemed to piss off the people of Iowa. I guess you couldn't blame them.

We persevered, although it is hard not to have a bad impression of a state when its residents don't like your message, or your dad.

What carried us through was an awareness of our strategy and that New Hampshire mattered in a way that Iowa didn't. There are lots of strategies for winning the presidency, of course. The all-time dumbest was Rudy Giuliani's in the last election. His tactic was to completely bypass Iowa, New Hampshire, and South Carolina and to concentrate on one thing: winning Florida. Because Florida has more electoral college votes than the first three states combined. But staying away from those early states means you don't have momentum and a domino effect going for you.

Some people thought Giuliani was crazy like a fox—and a bold experimenter with the basic game plan. But mostly what we talked about on our campaign was how tan Giuliani was. All the other presidential candidates were sallow and pasty from spending the fall and winter in New Hampshire and Iowa, but Giuliani had a tan to beat all tans. In the end, that's all he had.

8

LIVE FREE OR DIE

ALL THE OLD DUDES IN POLITICS, THE DIEHARDS AND POLITICAL LIFERS WHO HAD WORKED ON SEVEN AND EIGHT PRESIDENTIAL CAMPAIGNS ALREADY, had advised me not to get too emotionally invested in anything—campaign friendships, campaign staff, the places where we traveled, or even the outcome of each election. If you get invested, they said, it meant you were vulnerable to discouragement, upsets, and meltdowns—things that can mess with your sense of direction and focus. But I found all of this impossible as soon as I got to New Hampshire.

To me, the state is surrounded in a golden haze, and my memories from there are like a beautiful dream. I'm sorry, Iowa, but I get wistful when I think of New Hampshire, and teary-eyed, and maudlin. There's no emotional distance for me, or restraint. Every day there felt unblemished, pure, organic, and wholesome—and every second made a mark on me in a powerful way. New Hampshire is where I fell in love with politics, head over heels.

The beauty of the state is incomparable, to begin with. I had seen it in autumn, for some early campaigning before primary season, when the landscape glowed with color—red and orange and yellow—and the sharp sunlight was golden. And later, just before the New Hampshire primary in January, it was bitter-ass freezing, so cold that my body was screaming, but, at the same time, it was so magical, so clean, an amazing winter wonderland.

Growing up in Arizona, we weren't a skiing family and never went to snowy places. When Christmas vacation came every year, my parents took all of us to an island in the South Pacific for a week, a sunny resort where my mom and dad had been going for years, since before we were born. And although I had gone to college in the Northeast and had certainly experienced snow, I had never really seen it fall like that outside of New York City. I had never seen the way it settles on a small town, or covers a forest in white. For me, there is nothing like it.

And the people of New Hampshire are just as amazing. Unlike the Iowans, who didn't care much for my dad, the people of New Hampshire couldn't get enough of him. Maybe they just couldn't get enough of politics. They are more active and involved in the political process than quite possibly any other population in the United States. Because New Hampshire is "first in the nation"—meaning that it is the first state in the nation to hold a primary—it can really dictate how the season of primaries and possibly the election will go.

In other words, their votes truly count, and they feel it. In a day and age when it is so easy to become jaded or apathetic, and stay away from the democratic process of electing a president, the people of New Hampshire relish electing them. At times their enthusiasm was so intense, it was palpable and infectious. To this day, whenever I start to give up hope about America, I think of New Hampshire and the people there.

The town halls in New Hampshire start early, and in December 2007—a month before the primary—there were four of them, crammed with life and excitement, and a poignant small-town charm. One of them was attended by a white goat named Binx that everybody knew.

(There are zillions of photos of Binx online, and Beanie Babies of him.) It isn't unusual for a voter in New Hampshire to attend several town halls before deciding how to vote. People take their time and really ponder the issues—and hear firsthand how each candidate responds to a good grilling. My dad used to tell a joke on the stump about a barber in New Hampshire who asked another barber what he thought of Morris Udall—a one-time candidate for president also from Arizona—and the second barber said, "I don't know, I only met him twice."

The venues of the town halls change—from VFW halls to school auditoriums—but they all follow a similar format. A politician arrives, gets on a small stage with a microphone, and gives a speech about why he is the best candidate and should earn the people of New Hampshire's vote. After that, it's an open field. People stand up and ask whatever question they want. And ask they do. A town hall in New Hampshire can last several hours—something that used to drive my father's staff crazy. The questions vary wildly, from issue to issue, but share an underlying motivation: People need to be heard. They have problems and concerns and worries, and at the end of the day, they just want somebody to hear them.

It's no secret that President Obama is better than my father at delivering a speech. But nobody is better than my father at conducting a town hall. He loves the unplanned quality of it—the raw, uninhibited, unrestrained atmosphere. In the insanely controlled environment of politics today, my father loves the rare moment when almost anything can happen.

WHEN WE WERE IN NEW HAMPSHIRE, MOST OF THE time, we stayed at the Concord Marriott. There's nothing special about its appearance; it looks like every other Marriott in the world. People always complained that the bar closed at eleven, which seemed way too early for call time. But I loved it and, for me, it was really a second home. The bus would pick us up there in the morning and drop us off late at night. I ate every single snack offered—Snickers, Starburst, and soda—and tried almost everything on the menu in the small restaurant in the front. By the end of it, I am sure I memorized the options.

The owner of the Concord Marriott is Steve Duprey, a really decent guy, and one of my favorite people on the campaign. He was one of "the Originals," as we called them, people who believed in my dad since the very beginning. *Newsweek* had a nickname of its own for Duprey, "the court jester," because he was always handing out candy and joke gifts, my favorite of them all being shot glasses with the slogan "A straight shot on the Straight Talk Express."

On top of everything else, Duprey was a calming influence on my dad. He came along on campaign events, and often spent the day flying from event to event with my dad, and kept the vibe on the plane upbeat and light. He has a wild array of socks, too, which we documented on the blog regularly—socks with hearts and pigs with wings, and even socks with the Greek symbol for man, like Austin Powers uses. Every morning, a different pair. When I ran into him in the lobby, I'd ask Steve Duprey for a sock update. Heather would take pictures and we'd post them on the blog.

Shannon and Heather and I shared one room in those early days. At the Concord Marriott, we were in the back of the hotel, and we had a big window looking out on a small forest. Our room was crowded with our stuff—a total mess, totally trashed with blog equipment, photo stuff, cameras, and all our makeup, clothes, our huge suitcases. We were like animals, like bears who have to litter and mess up their cave to feel it is theirs. We used to joke that when we opened our suitcases, they would explode all over the room like those joke cans with spring-loaded snakes that come flying out of the top.

From the beginning, Shannon noticed that there were no other Asians in New Hampshire. It is kind of a homogeneous state. We always laughed about this together, but, at the same time, I did wonder if it bothered Shannon more than she said.

One day we were sitting in our hotel room, and feeling tired, and kind of worn down by the slog of the blog, by the meals that were starting to be predictable and not that healthy, by our lack of sleep—and maybe the bitter cold outside. Shannon made another joke about being the only Asian in New Hampshire, and this time, I kind of felt it, and worried.

Just then, as we were looking out the big window of our room—literally five minutes after Shannon admitted that she felt out of place—an Asian family appeared and ran out into the snow and started making a snowman.

We jumped up and down, screaming and laughing. That's what I mean when I tell people that New Hampshire is a magic place. As if the Granite State hears your wishes and makes them come true.

ONE OF THE WEIRDEST THINGS ABOUT OUR POLITICAL process is that some candidates really come out of nowhere. Now, I give it up to anyone who wants to make a go at becoming president—just trying, just going through the ordeal. It is an intense process and very stressful no matter what level you get to. And there was a time when my dad was an out-of-left-fielder. When he first ran for president in 2000, he had 5 percent name recognition with a 5 percent margin of error, meaning that it was possible that nobody in the state of New Hampshire knew who he was.

Mike Huckabee had come from left field in 2007—and the former governor of Arkansas had gone on to win in Iowa and become a force to be reckoned with in the primaries. But there were other candidates who came from left field and remained there. Their ability to persevere was remarkable. I suppose it is the essence of the American dream to be a total unknown and eventually become president. But I just couldn't help but wonder why some of them ran in the first place—other than trying to increase their name recognition, or perhaps they were bored and needed a thrill.

And then there was Fred Thompson, the well-known former senator and TV star of *Law & Order*. His bizarre presidential campaign in 2008 provided the opposite scenario. He was famous and well known, and was talked about as a player. But he didn't seem interested in trying at all, let alone persevering. Why was he running? His primary schedule was so lackluster, it was laughable. Reporters and campaign staff used to follow it online for comic relief.

Two other Republicans mystified me. They seemed to have absolutely no hope of making it to the convention. Duncan Hunter was a congressman from California; Tom Tancredo was a former congressman from Colorado. Neither of these men seemed to have a following that was growing, as far as anybody could tell. Yet there they were, week after week, appearing at debates, waiting around afterward for somebody to show up and shake their hands or want their picture.

Duncan Hunter always seemed like a nice man. What kind of wild confidence kept him going? On primary day in New Hampshire, when I was riding in a cavalcade of buses from rally to rally with my dad, we stopped at a red light and I saw Duncan Hunter across the street, on a corner of the intersection. He was standing with his wife and maybe two other people. He was holding a sign that said "Duncan Hunter for President."

It was admirable he was still out there, campaigning until the bitter end. And I remember thinking how nice it was that he was keeping it old-fashioned, old-school, with his handheld sign.

But I also remember thinking, no matter what happens in this election, nothing could be worse than being Duncan Hunter today. And at the same time, what hope! What optimism! It was easy to be cruel and make Duncan Hunter jokes. I will spare you those. My heart goes out to a guy who can do that.

ELECTION DAYS CAN BE BORING. YOU'VE WORKED HARD, gone full bore—have shed lots of campaign blood, sweat, and tears—

and then election day comes and you sit around and wait. The voting booths don't close until very late. So you wait for exit polls that come around four in the afternoon.

The day before, we'd done a long, multi-stop bus tour around the state—my mom, Bridget, Heather, Shannon, and I, and a full bus of campaign staff. We started at seven in the morning and ended at ten that night. We went from rally to rally, the momentum building as the day wore on. The energy was electric; people screaming, holding signs, hugging, yelling, crying. It was unbelievable, as if people at the rallies were watching their hopes and dreams for the future manifest themselves in their candidate. By the end of that day, I could barely move and fell asleep at the hotel in my clothes and makeup, something I hadn't done since I was a freshman at Columbia.

The next morning I slept in late, and woke up to the TV news going with reports from the precincts that were open. I finally showered and got in my jammies and UGG boots, still trying to recover from the mad campaigning of the day before. Pajamas are particularly good for the limbo of an election day, because deep inside, what you really want to do is go back to bed and wake up when it's all over.

To kill time that afternoon, a bunch of us went to Tortilla Flat, the Mexican restaurant outside of Nashua where I'd eaten eight years before, when my father won the primary. It seemed like a great idea, and would maybe bring us good luck. I remember it was really snowy and beautiful and that I went out with a coat thrown over a pair of leggings and a sweater, and didn't bother putting any makeup on. I was so happy not to have to get up at the crack of dawn and be a daughter-of prop who waved in a cute outfit.

After lunch, on the way back to the hotel, we noticed a street corner with a bunch of Mitt Romney signs. His signs were everywhere, wherever you looked in New Hampshire. I'd gotten pretty sick of them. Somebody from the Romney campaign had even put a ton of their signs right outside our campaign hotel too, knowing that we were all inside and forced to look at them. So when we saw a bunch of Romney signs on that corner on election day, and nobody else was around, we asked our driver to pull over. We got out of the car and walked over to the signs—planning to put them all in our trunk.

Stealing campaign signs is technically illegal, but I never thought anyone would enforce this. Nor did I expect we'd get caught. But just as we had pulled over and I had shoved a ton of Romney signs into our trunk, another car pulled up and blocked us. A super-dorky guy in a suit leaped out of his car. He was pissed as hell.

"What campaign are you with?" he yelled.

"Giuliani," we said.

He pulled out a notepad and proceeded to take down our license plate number. This is when I started freaking out. "MCCAIN DAUGH-TER ARRESTED" was the headline that I saw in my head.

Getting arrested on the day of the New Hampshire primary?

Oh, man. I imagined the look on my mom's face.

If only we could get away.

"Please move your car," I said to the guy, hoping to bully him a little.

He was such a jerk. And when he wouldn't move his car, my heart started to race and I was afraid for a minute that I might do something even worse than stealing a bunch of Romney signs. But anybody who was lame enough to pull over and harass people on election day for stealing signs was probably lame enough to follow up and bring some New Hampshire state troopers to arrest me.

As soon as he pulled away, we sped back to our hotel, where I tracked down Piper Baker, my mom's hairstylist. Piper and I look alike. We really do. Well, sort of. I had a plan. If the police traced the car to our campaign, could Piper say that she stole the signs and not me?

Good ol' Piper. She was game. "So long as your mom doesn't fire me," she said.

"No, no, no. That will never happen," I promised.

Then I went to Joe Donahue, a campaign aide who is like a brother to me, and a longtime friend of my dad's, and made a full confession. I had to tell somebody what had happened. "I could get arrested, Joe," I kept saying. "I could. I could. What should I do?"

"You'll be okay," he kept answering, over and over. And he was right. The state troopers didn't come.

But I guess I should admit that, as the campaign wore on, this wasn't the only time Piper came in handy as my stunt double. I am amazed how many journalists thought she was me, let alone supporters and volunteers. Looking back on it, though, I think it would have been pretty damn funny to get arrested for stealing signs on election day, although I'm not sure my parents would have bailed me out.

AT 8:15 THAT NIGHT, I WAS IN MY DAD'S PRIVATE HOTEL room with my family and a few journalists when his victory was declared. The room exploded in cheers and screams. All the noise in the world seemed like silence to me, compared to the way I felt inside. I used to say that I wanted a tattoo that said "Live Free or Die" on my arm. My feelings of relief and gratitude—love—for the people of New Hampshire were suddenly too great to keep in. I cried and hugged everyone in sight.

Just six months before, our campaign had been broke, understaffed, and declared dead. To win now seemed nothing short of a miracle.

Victory of this kind is hard to describe, but once you've experienced it, and been part of an underdog operation that comes from behind and rushes to triumph, you know why people devote their lives to politics, to fighting for issues they believe in, to the exhilarating battle of wits and skill and experience that make up a presidential campaign. I felt so buoyant, alive, and filled with a wild sense of accomplishment and reward.

The slate had been cleaned. My dad was now the front-runner. The happiness I felt was breathtaking. But underneath, there was sadness, too. Because I sensed that it was the last night of the good old campaign days—the small towns, the snowy landscape, the feeling of being surrounded by goodwill and peace.

As the months passed, and we kept winning—twenty-two primaries in two months—we used to half-jokingly say, "I miss New Hampshire." For a while, we talked about putting that phrase on a T-shirt. We didn't. But the feeling never went away.

9

ROYAL WHITE HOUSE MESS

LET ME BEGIN THIS STORY ABOUT GOING TO THE WHITE HOUSE TO MEET FORMER FIRST LADY LAURA BUSH AND FORMER FIRST DAUGHTER JENNA, BY admitting that I have always had insecurities about being an inadequate daughter-of. I am always afraid that people expect me to be milder, quieter, and more composed, like the other daughters-of.

Being a daughter-of is a weird little club, if you think about it. And membership comes with a weird little celebrity. Your parents are in the limelight, and like it. But this doesn't mean you will too. It is hard to tell how the other daughters-of are dealing with this, because many of them seem to be kind of shut down. Since your entire job in public life is standing, waving, and wearing the right clothes, you can become a permanent cardboard figure, I guess, like a princess doll. And since the world can be focused on you, and fascinated, maybe it seems safer to say nothing.

I might be the only member of the club who doesn't have a problem talking like this. So many of the other daughters-of are shy and private, but that's essentially the exact opposite of who I am. And it is one reason why, when I'm around other daughters-of, I feel like the odd girl out, like the zebra in a room full of leopards. I look different too. I like to wear my hair super-long and as blond as possible. And sometimes, I admit, I get carried away with makeup. My personal style can come off a little more like Gwen Stefani than Tricia Nixon Cox.

I always have wanted a group of daughters-of to get together and lock the door, share experiences and secrets. But I don't think there is really any chance of that happening. The others are so composed and discreet—and almost seem to be waiting for somebody to peel them a grape.

WHEN I FOUND OUT THAT MY MOM AND I WERE IN-vited to go to the White House for lunch I immediately became anxious. To be honest, it wasn't thoughts about the South Carolina primary in 2000 that got me in a state. My first concern was totally my wardrobe.

I had been on the road for two weeks at the time my mom got the invitation—and there was nothing clean left in my suitcase. I was at the point in my campaign laundry cycle where I was rewearing bras and leggings, a gross necessity when you are living out of a suitcase for days at a time. I love how the words "I'm on the road" sound so sexy and alluring when they are coming out of a woman's mouth, and sometimes when I said it myself, I felt like Penny Lane, the super-cool girl on the bus in *Almost Famous*. But the realities of road life weren't so glamorous.

To begin with, I was hanging out with old Republican men with hygiene deficiencies, not rock stars. And rather than wearing a big fur coat and bell bottoms, I was lugging around a suitcase of stained tops and grungy purple tights.

What the hell do I wear to the White House?

Just two days before, my dad had won the Republican primaries in Ohio, Texas, Vermont, and Rhode Island—and had locked up the party nomination. He was going to the White House himself to be endorsed by the president, a final burying-of-all-remaining-hatchets ceremony in the Rose Garden.

The next day, my mom and I were invited for lunch there. It was pitched as a "get-to-know-you" visit, a passing of the torch sort of thing. After all, it was no longer unimaginable that we'd be living there in less than a year. For me, it was exciting to have a chance to see it, finally, up close. I had only been there once, when I was ten or eleven, on a public tour during the Clinton years. But I'd never seen the residence before.

I was really excited to meet Laura and Jenna Bush too. Jenna always seemed so fun, from everything I had read about her. She had recently become engaged and there had been a number of stories about it. She seemed to be turning into a less private daughter-of, somebody who was becoming more comfortable with attention and publicity. When I thought of meeting her, I imagined us sitting down in a private corner of the White House residence together, sharing tales and swapping brand names of our favorite blush. I envisioned a totally girly moment, to be honest. I have always wanted to bond with another daughter-of, and have one for a friend.

Shopping in a hurry has never been one of my strengths. I wind up with the wrong things, inevitably. After rushing around Georgetown in a frenzy, desperate to find something appropriate, I decided on a black, knee-length Diane von Furstenberg dress with a black sash around the waist and a little black cotton jacket/poncho to go over it. I also found a pair of patent leather round-toe Tory Burch shoes with black glitter on the heel to spice up the outfit a bit.

I couldn't go wrong with that, I thought. Black is my favorite color—my signature, if you will. And Diane von Furstenberg seems to work in literally every social setting I can imagine—from a night in a crummy bar to a trip to the White House.

The next morning, I woke up early and got started on my hair. I asked Piper, my mom's hairdresser, to braid my hair into three rows flat on my head. I was aiming for a fusion of African cornrows and a crazy blond look that Piper and I had devised earlier in the year.

Cornrows really worked on the road, in any case. It was a great way to have my hair out of my face, and pulled up, but not too old or serious looking.

Shannon and Heather were coming along, and we had called the First Lady's office and had been told that they could bring their cameras—which seemed so cool of the White House. But about thirty minutes before we left the hotel, my mom's assistant got another phone call. No cameras allowed.

Fine, I thought. And I understood that cameras may seem intrusive. It irritated me at the same time—these last-minute changes were a daily problem on the campaign. We were allowed access, and then, at the last minute, we'd get a call saying we weren't. I hated the drama, and the indecisiveness.

We all piled into one of those giant SUVs that the Secret Service used to drive my parents around. My mom looked really pretty in a gray suit with her hair pulled half up and half down. She always knows exactly what to wear, and how to pull an outfit together and make it look seamless. It's a talent that I wish I had.

Another thing about my mom: No matter what I'm wearing, she always says I look great.

NOW, I DON'T CARE WHO YOU ARE, OR HOW LUXURIOUS and rarified your background is, the White House is spectacular. Just driving through the gates makes you giddy, it just does. The lawns are a perfect green with perfect hedges. The building is huge and white and spectacularly beautiful. It doesn't seem real. It looks like a movie set or a palace.

At one of the side entrances, our car was met by the First Family's small dogs who were scrambling around. When I knelt down to pet one, the dog growled at me. It should have been a warning sign of things to come.

First impressions count for a lot. We were met by a White House aide, who greeted us and shook everyone's hand but Shannon's. Was this an accident? I don't know. But it was very uncomfortable, for us, anyway, that the one minority standing in line with all of us didn't get welcomed or greeted, as though she wasn't a real guest. Maybe because Shannon looks really young she was consciously, or unconsciously, deemed unworthy. But I immediately felt bad about it, and sorry that I couldn't step in and say something. To say something would have made it worse.

We were led down a long corridor and then up in an elevator to the East Wing, I believe, but it was all so beautiful and surreal I can't remember exactly where we were. The elevator was wooden on the inside, and very elegant. I looked over at Shannon and giggled when she mouthed the words, "what the fuck?" I knew that she was referring to the fact that she wasn't greeted. But soon enough, the doors opened.

Now, the White House, although gorgeous and stunning, is a lot smaller inside than I imagined. Looking at the exterior of the building, you would expect the spaces inside to be soaring. But instead, it feels cozy and intimate. We entered a room with a big oval window where the sun shined in and flooded a giant plush couch with warm light. The glossy wooden floors creaked when I walked on them, and there were beautiful old colonial paintings on the walls, and giant tapestries. Sitting on the big tables were enormous bouquets of yellow roses, and their amazing fragrance filled the room. It was just surreal and wonderful.

While Heather and Shannon talked with an aide, my mom and I sat down on the big cushy couch and waited.

Laura Bush arrived, greeted us in her cool but warm way. She was wearing black slacks, a black sweater, and black ballet flats, and looked very nice, but much more casual than I expected. From television and magazine pieces about her, I had come to assume she wore a bright red pantsuit and full face of camera-ready makeup wherever she went. Also, the surroundings of the White House are so grand and formal, it was a little disorienting to see her so relaxed. But here, she was in her own home, after all.

At night, did she walk around in sweatpants? Thinking about this was like being at Disneyland and wondering what happened when all the tourists are gone. It made me giggle. In my mind, even at night-time at the White House, people should be wearing giant silk robes and golden slippers. Anything else would spoil the mood.

We all sat down and made small talk. I don't remember what we talked about, it was chitchat—about being from Texas and Arizona, campaigning, the Republican Party . . . nothing incredibly memorable. I am not sure what I expected, maybe just a more friendly and inclusive person, full of warmth, the way her voice sounds on TV. But being sensitive and instinctual, I pick up on vibes, body language, and body signals to an excruciating degree. And there was no doubt in my mind that, for Mrs. Bush, this was just one more meeting she had to take during the day. I tried not to take it personally, and I'm sure my mom didn't either.

Jenna showed up soon enough, just back from a shopping trip. I was surprised by how petite she is, short and very thin. She wore long slacks, a gray quarter-length sweater, a long jacket, and ballet slippers. Head to toe, she was just beautiful and casually elegant. And suddenly it was hard not to feel a little bit stupid in my glitter heels and corn-rows. What was I thinking?

Jenna was very friendly and we slipped quickly into small talk, not really banter. Henry Hager, her fiancé—now her husband—was with her, an extremely tall guy with a smooth look and manner, pretty much what you'd expect from a Maryland tobacco heir. Then the First Lady and Jenna took us on a short tour of the White House.

The Lincoln Bedroom, while not enormous, is really beautiful—all wood, an old bed, big windows, and it is amazing when you are inside it to imagine Abraham Lincoln really sleeping there. It had just been refurbished, and recently photographed for a magazine, so every detail was perfect and breathtaking. I have a pretty sizable fascination with Abraham Lincoln that borders on worship, and I felt overwhelmed, suddenly. He is my favorite president. I had a funny time-traveling feeling: "I'm standing in the Lincoln freaking bedroom!!!"

Jenna took us to see her bedroom, which conjoined the one that her sister, Barbara, used. I was shocked at how small it was—really, it was the size of a dorm room, and pretty unremarkable, on the order of a charming room in an old bed-and-breakfast inn. On the wall, I remember there was a creepy painting of two celestial babies—twins—that scared me. I zeroed in on a super-small flat-screen television, but aside from that, I didn't have one single feeling of excitement that someday, maybe in less than a year, this could be my bedroom. But since I wasn't planning on living with my parents, anyway, I wondered how I'd break the news to Bridget.

It was time for lunch, and this is where my White House visit becomes a little strange. Apparently there had been some miscommunication between the First Lady's office and my mother's personal assistant, because, in fact, the actual invitation for lunch was extended to my mother only—and not me.

Standing there, I was suddenly so embarrassed that I didn't know what to say, except, "That's fine, fine, okay, whatever." The sort of thing anybody would say under those circumstances. I sputtered out some jokes, but it was impossible to not feel like my very presence was somehow now a big problem. "Sorry, I'm a White House party crasher!" I wanted to say. But in all my embarrassment, and self-focus, it didn't occur to me how odd it was that Mrs. Bush or her social office didn't simply enlarge the lunch table to include me, or at least make more of an effort to have me feel less weird.

An aide of Mrs. Bush's was standing by, and suggested that Jenna and I have lunch in something that she called "the White House mess." I thought that sounded cool, some crazy "mess hall" in the White House—and imagined a big, army-style cafeteria with plastic trays and good chocolate pudding in swirly goblets, maybe even that fake whipped cream. And maybe there, I imagined, Jenna and I could have our girls' gabfest, and gossip more freely about the hilarious demands of being a daughter-of.

"The mess?" Jenna asked dismissively. "What's that? I've never heard of it."

She laughed nervously and I could see she wasn't happy.

Now, if you are me and you have serious insecurities about not being refined enough, elegant enough, or basically quiet and calm enough to have a place within the small circle of political daughters-of, this was my nightmare. Somehow, by just showing up, I had irritated Jenna and put Mrs. Bush and her staff in an uncomfortable position of wondering what to do about me, where to put me, and how to feed me.

Jenna and Henry bowed out of any lunch plans, as quickly as possible, and began to say their good-byes. They were in the middle of planning their wedding, after all, and had things to do. There was a brief conversation about the sick stuff that people post on the Internet, and I made a quip about these things being written by "guys who live in their mothers' basements and have nothing else to do." I was happy when Jenna and Henry laughed at that, and the air became less heavy in the room.

Mrs. Bush's aide kindly stepped in, and offered to take me to lunch with Shannon and Heather. The aide was perfectly nice and pleasant, but her entire conversation was about her new Smart Car and how excited she was to own one. She seemed so thrilled with herself and delighted by her new car—and talked incessantly about the joys of her new vehicle as we made a long journey outside the building and down sets of stairs to another wing of the White House.

THE WHITE HOUSE MESS DIDN'T LOOK ANYTHING LIKE I'd pictured. Like I said, my image was of a "mess hall" or an army cafeteria. But the one in the White House, although in the basement, is a gorgeous dining room with waiters and beautiful flowers, where, it turned out, the senior staff of the White House eat lunch and are treated like members of a small private club. The interior of the mess is designed to look like the captain's quarters on a ship, with wood tables and chairs, and various nautical touches. The walls are covered with black-and-white photos.

How could Jenna Bush have not heard of this place—or been here? If my dad were president of the United States, I would be here all the time, I thought, and it would really make up for the little bedroom. It was like a secret clubhouse!

Plates of food being carried from the kitchen looked incredible, and smelled even better. The White House kitchen has an amazing reputation and I could tell that lunch was going to be spectacular, I just knew it, and couldn't wait.

We sat down at a table, and were joined by another aide or staffer. The conversation about Smart Cars continued, to the point of mind-numbing tediousness, and I do remember having a brief out-of-body experience, and laughing to myself. It was so typical that I would be here, at the White House, bullshitting with people, and blabbing about Smart Cars, when hypothetically I could be the First Daughter ten months from now.

Why did this seem like the story of my life? Or maybe it is just the story of a daughter-of's life. Maybe it wasn't about the Bushes and how they felt about me, or my dad. Maybe it didn't really matter who my dad was. At that moment, I was just along for the ride, a "family member" to chat up and an extra mouth to feed.

Except . . . I didn't get fed. Yep, the sad ending to this story about my visit to the White House is that our food didn't come in time. My mother and Mrs. Bush must have inhaled their meal in record time, because almost as soon as we ordered lunch in the mess, we were called away. My mom was ready to leave.

I was given a doggie bag of enchiladas instead.

Woof-woof.

Wanna talk about feeling stupid and unwanted? Try carrying a take-out bag as you leave the White House in sparkly glitter heels and your hair braided in three huge cornrows.

My mother met us outside, standing beside the big Secret Service SUV. She saw my doggie bag and looked confused.

"You haven't eaten yet?"

I shook my head. "Why couldn't you have taken longer with Mrs. Bush?"

My mom just stared at me. It wasn't the moment for rehashing. Once we were inside the car, I asked, "What did you and Mrs. Bush talk about?"

"Being First Lady," she said, and went into a bit more detail, but Mom being Mom was much more interested in what had happened to us. We couldn't have been off the grounds of the White House too long before we were all belly-laughing—Shannon and Heather and I fighting for a chance to describe how we'd *almost* eaten. Over the next few days, we managed to turn it into sketch comedy, acting out our parts and having great fun laughing about it. A sense of humor will get you through almost anything, even what was one of the most bizarre experiences of the campaign for me.

It felt so fitting, a perfect metaphor for how I felt about my place within the Republican political establishment too. It seemed like a place of almost cultish exclusivity. I was excited to be there, but they weren't excited to have me. For all intents and purposes, I should be allowed in and asked to join the team, but I am not invited, not asked to join, and in fact, even if I am allowed inside, I am relegated to the basement where I won't actually be given food.

I hope Laura and Jenna Bush won't be angry with me for dishing like this. But I use Taylor Swift as a model: if you don't want her to write a song about you, don't give her a reason.

There is a nice ending to the story, though. I'd like to make a promise to all future daughters-of—no matter how many years go by or whatever your political views—if you want to gab, share stories, bond, and have lunch, please give me a call. I promise to answer your questions, share my waving technique and other tricks I have picked up, give you a decent meal, and maybe gossip a little. Like Alice Roosevelt Longworth used to say: "If you haven't got anything nice to say about anybody, come sit next to me."

10

GENTLE FOLK OF THE MEDIA

A *GQ* PIECE ABOUT ME LANDED ON THE NEWS-STANDS TEN DAYS AFTER THE WHITE HOUSE VISIT. NEWS OF IT SWEPT THROUGH THE CAM-paign staff like wildfire and my phone never stopped ringing. Everybody wanted to tell me—in case I didn't already know—what I'd done wrong. Emotions weren't just running high. They were bouncing and pinging, ricocheting like atoms splitting inside a nuclear reactor.

If you track down the piece on the Internet now, it won't seem shocking or make me appear to be as maniacally stupid as it did at the time. That alone is a lesson in context. The backdrop of a presidential campaign has a way of magnifying and distorting all flaws, all bumps, anything out of the ordinary.

But I didn't feel out of the ordinary. I felt like an ass.

Normally, I am not big on the concept of regret. Or I should say that I don't believe in sitting around wallowing and wishing things were different. It's a cliché, but true, that we learn some of the most important things in life by our failures and mistakes. If we never had things that we were sorry we'd done, or sorry we'd said, we would never be forced to take a hard look at ourselves—and make changes for the better.

Even so, I regret just about everything that I was quoted as saying to the *GQ* reporter, regret spending hours alone with him, regret going bowling with him, regret hugging him good-bye (WHAT WAS I THINKING???), and, most of all, regret allowing the magazine to photograph me working on my laptop while sitting on top of a bed with an open bottle of Bud Light in my hand.

Mistakes were made, is what I want to say. And I learned from every single one.

THE BLOG WAS GATHERING STEAM—AND REACHING A mini boiling point that spring. A number of newspapers had written about it, and political sites had started linking to it regularly. Our regular audience was growing. Obviously, the fact that my dad was winning put me and the blog in the spotlight. After the New Hampshire primary, we had a great stretch of victories. Suddenly the media world was noticing everything we did and said.

Steve Schmidt acted surprised each time we won—which irritated me, I have to admit. He was so hard-bitten and lacking in joy. But I suppose his pessimism was a leveler, and kept people focused. For my family and me, the win in South Carolina was particularly sweet. The voters were gracious and warm and softened the bitter memories of what had happened eight years before. I was able to see that it wasn't the state or the people of South Carolina that had caused so much pain and disappointment for my dad and all of us. In a way, the smear of 2000 had tarnished the South Carolinians even more than it had my dad—and made them look like mudslinging racists, ignorant and pliable, when the spirit of the state is infectiously warm and generous and kind.

The night of our victory in South Carolina, I jumped around so much during the mass celebrating that the heel of my boot came off.

An incredible party ensued at the hotel where the campaign was staying—the most fun primary party of all. Nobody wanted to break it up and head to dinner, so Piper placed a four-hundred-dollar pizza order to be delivered to the lobby of our hotel.

After Super Tuesday in March, when my father won in Ohio, Texas, Rhode Island, and Vermont and gathered enough electoral votes and delegates to be the Republican nominee, the campaign regrouped— shifting its focus from worrying about Romney and Huckabee to worrying about the Democrats, and trying to calculate who would be our likely rival in the fall.

It was going to be a tough race. Not much disagreement about that.

The race between Hillary Clinton and Barack Obama was still heated and close. Hillary was winning important states, and to me, she seemed like the one to beat. She was becoming more formidable and a better campaigner with each primary. As a woman, I have to admit that I admired her dogged energy and amazing encyclopedic brain. She won all the debates, as far as I was concerned, while Obama always seemed out of his depth and foggy. Every time Hillary opened her mouth, even if she wasn't actually saying something serious, she seemed impressive, so articulate and razor sharp.

Being in public life for decades can cripple your spirit—and spoil your spontaneity and openness. I had learned that much from my short life in politics. That's why so many politicians seem shut down and barely present. Something inside is gone, or no longer accessible. I liked Hillary Clinton but also felt bad for her. I couldn't help but wonder about all the parts of herself that she had deep-sixed just to keep herself attractive to voters. Maybe my instincts are off about her, but I doubt Hillary really cares about clothes and fashion. It seems almost tragic when I think about all of the hours of her life that she's had to devote to these things, when she has other matters she's much more passionate about.

Political life is rough on women, whether you are a wife or daughter or candidate yourself. After eight months on the road, I understood that in ways that I never had before. It made me much more sympathetic to my mom and other political wives—as well as the women who join campaigns to work as high-ranking staffers. You have to be pretty tough to hack it. If you could do guy-talk, and shoot the shit about sports—*men's teams,* of course—that was even better.

Looking around my dad's campaign, it was painfully obvious that politics was dominated and organized by guys. Some of them were nicer than others. Some were more cultured and better educated than others. But whether they were hanging out together, or doing business, they bonded over guy stuff, football and college basketball—stuff that has never interested me for a second.

If you were a woman and wanted to be heard, and taken seriously, you were better off acting like a guy. And no matter what, you couldn't show any emotion unless it was anger. But not when TV cameras were around.

On camera, and onstage, women in politics weren't supposed to seem angry, ever. You had to seem soft, sweeter than a guy, compassionate, and at least believably maternal. My mom was all of those things—super-maternal and feminine—but when she got on a stage or gave an interview, she shut down. It was hard for her to open up. I guess you can't blame her. But it made me sad to see that she didn't trust or connect with the media. Reporters who couldn't feel her warmth and big heart assumed these things weren't there.

When Hillary Clinton shed a tear in New Hampshire, and again on the eve of Super Tuesday, I was impressed that she had let down her guard—and shown what was really going on inside. She was suddenly human, and a woman. The male journalists described it as though she had been sobbing and out of control, when in fact her eyes had just welled up. And when she took a shot of Crown Royal whiskey at Bronko's Restaurant in Indiana—putting it back just like a guy—I was stunned by the media fascination with it. Every pundit had a comment. The blogs went nuts and the video went viral. *A woman having a shot of whiskey?* Was this kind of thing allowed?

I was sure that being a man had made things easier on my dad. Not that running for president is a laugh riot. But at least he never had to worry about the shape of his legs, how big his ass was, or whether he was having a bad hair day—the sorts of things that women in public life are routinely pummeled for, if they aren't paying enough attention to their appearance.

How much time had Hillary Clinton spent considering her outfits and accessories for debates—or sitting in a salon chair getting her hair done? My dad didn't have things like that to worry about.

Not that he was on easy street. After forty-seven years of serving his country—twenty-four years in the House and Senate, twenty-three years in the U.S. Navy—he had a promising chance of becoming the president of the United States. The stakes were daunting, dizzying. When I thought about it, what he was facing, and taking on, I was amazed by him. He was so strong, and ready for all of it. But the stress was intense. He once told me that he thought the pressures of a national campaign were on par with the pressures of war.

Dad seemed unfazed by the hot glare of media. From what I could see, he had barely switched gears. He was up to the challenge, and the job.

But how ready was I?

WHEN *GQ* CALLED AND ASKED FOR AN INTERVIEW, I didn't flatter myself that it was really about me—or I tried not to. The campaign was winning, after all, which made my whole family more media-worthy. My younger brothers, Jack and Jimmy, were both in the military, which forbade them, for the most part, from giving interviews. My sister, Bridget, was too young, from my parents' point of view, to be in the spotlight. My dad's sons and daughter from his first marriage, Doug, Andy, and Sidney, were busy professionals with their own lives and families. I was the lone McCain kid on the road, and visible. I didn't know a thing about giving an interview, but I was eager to help my dad in any way I could.

Political kids are supposed to be an asset, which is why campaigns usually find ways to expose them, even exploit them, in order to humanize the candidate. Kids remind the world, and the voters, that—no matter how canned and phony a politician may seem—he or she is a real person with real stuff going on.

My dad's campaign seemed a little slow to jump on board with the family stuff. Even at the beginning of the summer going into the convention, I remember reading a poll showing that a majority of voters didn't realize my dad had children—and although they must have assumed he was married, they didn't know much, if anything, about his wife.

My mom is private by nature and holds her cards close in a new situation. Once she warms up, she is almost as much of a free spirit as I am. Would voters ever get a chance to see that? Would a member of the media be able to see and describe her clearly, rather than just writing about her faraway stare?

As for me, I am not guarded by nature, and the prospect of being interviewed didn't make me too nervous. I assumed that all I had to do was "be myself" and the media would get me, and maybe even like me. That was basically my public relations strategy, anyway. Did I need media training? I didn't think so. Just the word *training* made me imagine being led around on a choke chain and leash by one of those weird dog handlers in the movie *Best in Show*. I didn't want to be a scripted daughter-of, or flatten myself into a boring cartoon.

If I kept it real and didn't bullshit people, I assumed that somehow I would be understood and appreciated.

Like I've said, I don't believe in secrets—or all the work that goes into trying to keep them. With me, what you see is what you get. Why should I act like somebody I wasn't? Being open and unguarded is how I have always made friends and bonded with people, even in work environments and paid internships. I believe that, at the end of the day, my personal connection with somebody is most important. It didn't occur to me that a relationship with a member of the media would be any different.

My mom and I didn't have a press person assigned to us, in any case. The campaign found us one after I screwed up, embarrassed everybody, and generated enough heat to set off all the campaign PR fire alarms.

THE YEAR BEFORE, SOME NEWSWEEKLIES HAD DONE roundups on the grown children of candidates who were working full-time on a campaign. These were ensemble pieces, each daughter or son getting a line or two of description, and maybe a quote. The Five Brothers would be grouped together, or the daughters like me, Cate Edwards, and Sarah Huckabee. We were all college-age or older, still single, and for the most part, on the road. Compared to Chelsea Clinton, a major celebrity who declined to participate in all interviews, or even talk to a ten-year-old reporter for *Scholastic,* we were all relative unknowns. In a group setting, the exposure for us was kind of gentle. The format didn't allow for media gotcha.

I'd already managed to embarrass myself, though. My first big on-camera interview was one of these group portrait pieces, by CBS News, about daughters-of. We were a campaign's "secret weapons," as the piece called us, and the story featured Sarah Huckabee, Cate Edwards, and me.

Cate Edwards looked gorgeous on camera, in her very East Coast way, with perfect straight brown hair, jeans, and suit jacket. She sounded even better—talking about how people relate to her, and in that way, relate to her father. Her ability to weave in the talking points of the Edwards campaign was stunning. To make the whole thing even more impressive, the backdrop of the interview was Harvard, where Cate was attending law school.

Then Sarah Huckabee came on-screen—and, like Cate, sounded and looked amazing. As I watched the piece, when it aired, I remember thinking how very classy she was in her suit and perfectly understated makeup. She talked about campaign strategy; she had been on the ground in Iowa, literally putting up signs and helping strategize.

Then . . . cut to me. I was wearing a knee-length black sequined skirt that looked way too glitzy, like it belonged on a Broadway stage. I was wearing *tons and tons* of makeup too—heavy eyeliner, layers of mascara, loads of blush. It took me a while to learn the art of applying makeup for TV and what I produced for that first interview was a recipe that would scare animals and small children.

Worst of all, every other word I said was *like*.

"Just because you, like, watch *The Hills*, doesn't mean, like, you can't, like, be involved in politics."

I giggled really fast, as if I were auditioning for a part in *Alvin and the Chipmunks*.

Like the nasty stream of online comments that my blog generated, the online reaction to the CBS interview was vicious—mostly about my *Hills* comment, and how bad my makeup was, and that I needed to stop bleaching my hair like a Vegas stripper. The other daughters were lauded—Cate for her brains, Sarah for her noble deeds, literally "out in the field" working for her dad.

I couldn't help but remember all the other things I had said to the reporter of the CBS interview, things that (in my memory, anyway) were smarter and less peppered with *like*s. The producers of the segment could have shown me in a better light—if they'd had a reason to. Maybe it was better television, better entertainment, to make me look like an idiot.

But did I have to make it so damn easy for them?

After all the money spent on my education, and hours studying at Xavier College Preparatory in Phoenix, a Catholic girls school, and later at Columbia University, and after all the various social and political events that I had been privileged to attend, and brilliant people

I'd been lucky enough to meet, you'd think that I could find a way to talk or dress like I'm not straight out of a mall in Scottsdale.

No offense, Scottsdale.

Malls either.

Well, you know what I mean.

THE *GQ* PIECE WAS ONLY A SHORT PROFILE—AND WAS going to run with a photograph of me. This didn't seem so hard, or complicated. The writer, a small guy who described himself as "nebbish" during the interview, flew to Phoenix to interview me. We talked for about an hour, drove to lunch at Garduno's Margarita Factory, and then we went bowling.

It seemed like my job was to provide him with as much information as possible, since he'd flown all the way to Arizona to see me, for God's sake. I had no idea that it was unusual for a candidate's daughter to be left alone for hours to gab with a feature writer. Nor did I expect that he would find a way to use every single semi-outrageous thing I said in order to make the piece as spicy and edgy as possible.

But if you are me, and you talk to somebody you like for four hours, you are going to wind up saying enough semi-outrageous things to fill up the entire issue of *GQ,* and maybe *Esquire* too. Even worse, when the magazine called to arrange a photo shoot, and I was on the road, it didn't occur to me that being photographed in my jeans and a black T-shirt on a hotel room bed with my computer on my lap and an open bottle of beer in my right hand, would make me look "slutty," as one staffer put it, or like one of those troubled political family members who is sliding down the slippery slope to catastrophic embarrassment.

What was forgotten—and left in the reporter's notepad and recorder—were hours of conversation about the campaign and my life outside of politics. The shreds of conversation that were used, babble and sputtering, became tantalizing nuggets. I made a remark that

Barack Obama was "sexy," said that I loved to watch a bisexual dating show on TV called *A Shot at Love with Tila Tequila*, and that I was a fan of the burlesque stripper Dita Von Teese.

A political gaffe is almost necessary in this kind of profile, apparently. I had unwittingly supplied that too. I said that I hoped Mike Huckabee wouldn't be my dad's running mate, and that he was better off running the evangelicals in the country instead.

Yes, I said all of those things. Mea culpa and all that. What is most noticeable is how painfully naïve I am in the interview, and how trusting. I thought the writer was just being really friendly and liked me, not just pretending that he did in order to manipulate me into providing juicy quotes. What a dope I was.

The cover of *GQ* said it all: "Is the White House ready for John McCain's daughter?" And the article was entitled "Raising McCain," a reference to the expression "raising Cain," meaning to raise hell, raise the devil, and basically cause drama.

Well, that much was true. The reaction to the *GQ* article was crazy. It was like that scene in the movie *Office Space,* when Ron Livingston's character gets inundated with e-mails and phone calls because he forgot to fill out his TPS report. Suddenly everyone in my path wanted to comment on my mistake and make sure I understood what I had done.

I was just twenty-three years old and had already won kudos for my blog, which I was funding entirely on my own, but suddenly the campaign was treating me like I was an irresponsible harlot who had released a sex tape with the president of Greenpeace.

When I look back on it now, it seems comical—as if my father wouldn't become president because of a story in *GQ* about me. The over-reaction was stunning. Even the word *irreparable* was used to describe the damage that I had caused. The interview was deemed "scandalous" and the accompanying photo was DEFCON 5 for headquarters.

I thought the piece was perfectly fine, when I first read it. But after hearing the reaction, I quickly descended into shame and apologized to my parents. Most of all, I took a giant red pill and woke up to reality. Most journalists only care about pleasing their editors, making a name for themselves, and coming up with the juiciest possible story. Maybe the collapsing industry of publishing has made things even worse—and journalists feel greater pressure to create sensationalized material.

Here's what I learned: Journalists do not care about the person being interviewed. And if they seem to, it's an act. So whatever happens, don't hug them good-bye.

The photograph still haunts me, not because I think I look that bad or trashy. It haunts me because I see a young girl, beautifully naïve and open and trusting, thinking that reporters are just people, just new friends.

I will never be that girl again.

First impressions are important. And the birth of my media persona wasn't so wonderful. Thousands of people were introduced to John McCain's daughter this way. I seemed to be a dummy with a big mouth and a beer bottle in her hand.

The funny thing is, I don't even drink much.

But I guess I do have a big mouth.

11

HOW THEY TRIED TO FIX ME

FOR A MONTH OR LONGER AFTER THE *GQ* PIECE, THERE WAS A "HOW DO YOU SOLVE A PROBLEM LIKE MARIA" MELODY SWIRLING AROUND ME, EXCEPT IT wasn't a bunch of nuns singing. It was the Three Groomsmen of the Apocalypse, as I had begun to lovingly call Steve Schmidt, Rick Davis, and Mark Salter. Looking back, I'm sure everybody meant well and cared only about winning.

I needed to be fixed—improved upon or polished up—or sent to Siberia. That was the basic message. The list of things that were wrong with me was growing. My hairstyles and taste in clothing were two strikes against me. I just didn't look anything like a Republican, which I was somewhat proud of. My tendency to swear was another.

Yes, I swear a lot. Especially if I am stressed out or hungry, which was, I have to admit, around the clock in those days. I apologize if I've become a huge disappointment in your eyes as a result of this confession, but if you could step inside the ramped-up environment of national politics, you'd know that foul language and swearing is as common on a presidential campaign as it is on a U.S. Navy battleship.

Even so, the ease with which I tossed F-bombs seemed as big an issue for my father's advisers as the economy. I wouldn't be surprised if there weren't a few meetings about it.

As far as the Three Groomsmen were concerned, I had become a political liability. Rather than helping my dad, I was informed that I was now hurting him.

When it comes to my dad, I'd do almost anything. If I could have morphed into another kind of daughter, I would have.

Toning down wasn't easy. What I needed was motivation—and fortunately, it came, suddenly, out of the blue.

A carrot was dangled in front of my face. I think it was my mom, or somebody on her staff, who mentioned to me that the campaign honchos were thinking about having me introduce Mom at the Republican convention. This news made my heart leap, and I gasped with delight.

Imagine that.

Speaking at the convention—a sea of people—millions of viewers all over the world. Me, on the convention stage. Me, introducing Mom.

I had never dreamed of an opportunity of this magnitude. Never in a million years. It was an incredible opportunity. Clearly it would be one of the most important and significant moments of my life.

My mom would love it too. She'd have a much easier time facing the convention crowd if I was there to introduce her, to give her a hug and cheer her on.

The prospect of this made me giddy, and each time I thought about it, my heart fluttered with excitement. More than anything, I wanted to be worthy and make everybody proud. I wanted to prove that everybody could put their faith in me—and not be disappointed. It was my big chance, let's face it: Finally I would ascend to respectable daughter-of-hood.

Whatever it took, I was game. Whatever suggestions the Groomsmen had, I would follow them.

So when word came down from campaign headquarters that I

should see a public speaking coach—a "media trainer"—and get a total overhaul by an image consultant, I didn't say no.

IT WAS SUMMERTIME AND WARM, JULY, WHEN I FLEW into Los Angeles for my big makeover. It was just a couple days, like media boot camp. The campaign had found a team of image consultants for me to see. It had also assigned a press secretary to my mom and me by then, a fantastic woman named Melissa Shuffield, who had worked in my dad's senate office. Tall, dark-haired, and striking looking, Melissa and I hit it off immediately. She is five years older than I and, like a lot of people that I gravitate to, she has a dry sense of humor and a no-drama personality. Some people invite drama in their lives. Some people always reject it. Melissa's equanimity was something that I would come to rely on and value in the rocky months ahead.

We drove to a large office space where two image consultants had set up business. It reminded me of Ari's office on the TV show *Entourage*, glassy and modern. There was a camera set up and a staging area with two director's chairs, where I sat for "mock interviews" that were taped and analyzed.

Outside, there was a Zen roof deck with pillows and lots of Buddhas around, where we went for breaks.

The consultants were two middle-aged women. One of them was super-attractive in a very Los Angeles kind of way, with short blond hair and camera-ready features. She was perfectly nice but, to be honest, it's hard to warm up to someone whose soul purpose is to analyze your "flaws."

The second consultant was a bit older, less done-up, and seemed more mellow. I guess I liked her a little more because, when they analyzed my hair, she was a lot nicer about it.

I wore a black button-down shirt and jeans to the meeting, trying to look as benign and toned-down as possible. Maybe that's why they began with my hair. The first consultant was highly critical. My hair was too blond and way too long. As soon as she started in, I had a paranoid fear that one of the Three Groomsmen had called beforehand and prepped her, because my "stripper" hair had been a subject of debate already on the campaign. The consultants actually referred to my hairstyle as "Brooke Hogan hair."

I'm not kidding. And was this such a terrible thing? Last time I checked, Brooke Hogan was gorgeous. But the consultants thought my hairstyle made me look slutty, unprofessional, and like the daughter of a professional wrestler, rather than the direct descendant of two four-star admirals and a legendary war hero who was now running for president.

My hair made me look slutty? This had never crossed my mind before. I had had super-long blond hair as long as I can remember, ever since I had dyed my hair deep red my freshman year of high school and let it fade. Afterward, I went blonder and blonder. I was a fan of Gwen Stefani, Marilyn Monroe, and Madonna—and I'd loved the way Carolyn Bessette Kennedy wore her hair—so bleached out and shiny. Obviously, even in high school I wanted to stand out and never saw anything wrong with that.

My hair is my security blanket. When it looks good, I feel good. That's true for lots of women. And I was attached to my long, bleached hair. But the image consultants clearly hated it—and changing my hair color and length became a priority.

I remember feeling self-conscious and kind of battered down, but trying to be good-natured about it. When I thought about the convention, just a month away, and introducing my mom (or my grandmother, as the campaign had recently mentioned), I agreed to allow the consultants to make an appointment with a salon in Beverly Hills where my hair would be fixed to become more appropriate and Republican looking.

If it meant less people on my ass, I would do it. I mean, it was only my hair, after all, and it would grow back.

Next, I sat down in front of the camera and gave a mock interview, which we watched later and analyzed. I was criticized for the way I talked. Apparently I have a scratchy Valley girl way of pronouncing things. I tried and tried to stop it and fix it. I was like Eliza Doolittle in *My Fair Lady*, sitting there with sentences to repeat, over and over. I failed every time. It was hard to drill all those *like*s out of me. So the consultants gave me "homework" to do—speaking exercises—to try to change that.

Also, I was a horrendous interview subject. I babbled on about things that I shouldn't have and needed to be more specific. I practiced that too.

My wardrobe was the next subject. On the campaign, I wanted to look like me—and pretty much wore my basic wardrobe of a big sweater and leggings, sometimes a dark dress with purple tights and some wild shoes. I am a shoe addict and I love fashion. Underneath it all, I should probably be a Vegas showgirl because I love accessories—bows and sequins, baubles and bangles, anything kind of glittery and bright.

And I love wearing over-the-top clothes when I can. When I was fifteen, and my dad was running for president for the first time, I wore a big poofy pink furry jacket everywhere. I was a little rebel. One of the staffers coined it "The Courtney Love Jacket." Looking back on it, it's kind of crazy that a fifteen-year-old was walking around in a pink furry coat. But my parents have always encouraged me to be myself, and look the way I want. When I am old, I hope that I can look like the designer Betsey Johnson—still working it, still out there, and wearing whatever I want.

According to the image consultants, though, I just looked terrible. They made an appointment for us to go to Neiman Marcus and shop for new clothes.

HOW WAS A WOMAN IN POLITICS SUPPOSED TO LOOK? I'D like to say that our audience is the general public, the man and woman on the street—the voters. In reality our audience is the media. And the media is very fickle. It can't decide how it wants a woman in politics to look.

Our country may honor individuality, but when it comes to a political figure, what's acceptable is narrow. How does a woman color inside the lines and still have her own personal style? It helps if the woman has pretty conventional taste to begin with—and can wear those clothes well. Aside from Jackie O and maybe Michelle Obama, I'm not sure if anyone has really mastered it yet.

I had already learned a few things by the time I got to the image consultant, though. Number one rule was not to show any skin—and to hide my boobs and body as much as possible. Early on, I was described in several articles as "voluptuous," which troubled me. Why describe my body at all? But my physical appearance was mentioned time and time again on the blogosphere. It seemed to surprise people that I wasn't dieting myself into oblivion or hiring a star personal trainer to get me ab'ed and muscled out. But I didn't want to diet and I didn't want to spend hours a day in a gym. And I didn't want to start looking less like a woman. I liked the way I was.

But for a woman in politics, revealing things that make you a woman is a total negative. No boobs. No ass. Not much leg. Bare arms, like Michelle Obama's, become a huge story.

If my brothers, Jack and Jimmy, had been working on the campaign, instead of me, would their appearance have been an issue? Would they have to hide their muscles and tattoos? Would the Groomsmen tell them to see an image consultant? And if they swore on the campaign bus, would anybody have noticed?

There's a double standard and I don't like it.

IN LOS ANGELES, UNDER THE SUPERVISION OF THE CON-sultants, my hair was chopped off to above my shoulders and their stylist put lowlights in my hair that looked like streaks of gray. I hated it immediately. But I swallowed my distress and didn't say anything, and wanted very much to embrace my new look. I made a few jokes that I had a "Fox News anchorwoman cut" but otherwise played along.

At Neiman Marcus, I got pantsuits. The consultants had made it clear, pretty much, that anybody in a pantsuit was brilliant and a woman in leggings and sweaters looked like a porn star. I didn't want to start wearing suits. But, again, I agreed. And with a little effort, I was able to find some edgy, fun suits that were cut well. I also discovered that in a pantsuit, it was easier to hide my ever-growing waist and ass. Ha!

And a few weeks later, I got a bill for thousands of dollars—the fee for the meeting with the image consultants and all their advice, not including the clothes I bought. Looking back, I am embarrassed that I went along with this and spent all that money of my own. It might have been one of the worst financial decisions I've made. But it taught me a lot about being true to myself, what I think is pretty, and what makes me happy in life.

I am happy being myself.

And I was happy to undo all the damage too. As soon as I returned to the campaign, I freaked out and had Piper dye my hair back to its old bleach-blond color. And I asked her to redo the haircut to something a bit edgier.

As far as my clothes, I continued to wear some suits and I might have toned down a bit too. Nothing else really changed. I still wore what I wanted. If anything, due to my newly conservative wardrobe, I began wearing more sparkly jewelry and Lucite bracelets and earrings. And while waiting for my hair to grow out, I began curling it and putting a little bow on the side, a look that I sort of stole from singer Katy Perry.

Little girls began showing up at my campaign events with the same look—curls with a bow on the side. It was so sweet. And I thought it was ironic that a look that I created in order to placate the Three Groomsmen became my "signature" campaign style. But as soon as the election was over, I never wore my hair like that again. It brought back too many memories. But I still have a giant box of all those bows in my closet at home.

I don't want to change. That's what I learned.

The Groomsmen were off my back, in any case. That's how it seemed. What I didn't realize was that they had a much bigger fish to fry. They were flying up to Wasilla, Alaska, and interviewing the governor there. They'd need to worry about how she looked too.

12

UN-CONVENTIONAL

THEY TELL ME THAT THE REPUBLICAN CONVEN-
TION WAS IN THE TWIN CITIES OF ST. PAUL–
MINNEAPOLIS. I DON'T HAVE ANY REASON TO
doubt that. But if you said we were in Kansas City or Kalamazoo, I
would believe that too.

It was a life indoors, a life unreal. My memories are dreamlike,
nightmarelike. I felt like I was underground—or trapped in a giant
closet. If there were windows, I never looked out of them. On my way
from one place to another, I had to tunnel through an obstacle course
of body traffic and security snafus. Passes weren't left for me, security
clearances were held up. Secret Service kept forgetting who I was. I
could have worn the special Secret Service pin that was given to "family
members" so they could be identified, but the pin bothered me and
kept damaging my tops, and I started feeling rebellious about it.

Forget the pin.

Remember my face.

Could you do that?

But that seemed too much to ask. Shannon and Heather and I

were always standing to the side, waiting to be cleared by security, or waiting for our passes to turn up. *Our names should be on that list. Can't you call somebody and clear us?* And the schedule kept changing. I would hear about an event I was supposed to attend after it had started. Or I would stand with wet hair at the door of the hair-and-makeup room, hoping for some help before a magazine shoot, but the chairs inside were filled by the Palin children. Even little Piper, age seven, was getting blowouts.

The weirdest thing was how time flew, like the convention was a black hole that sucked up all the minutes and hours around it. It sucked up all your sanity too. It is blurry now—a big, blank, blurry thing in my brain.

The weather seemed to manifest the swirl of chaos indoors. Hurricane Gustav was moving toward the Gulf of Mexico—a reminder of Katrina and how badly the disaster had been dealt with by a Republican administration. Not a good sign. I thought it was strange, and a little bit of poetic irony, that a natural disaster was going on, as if to remind us that no matter how prepared everyone tried to be for anything, the universe had other plans.

The announcement of Sarah Palin had thrown me off course. I was still reeling from the news and was fighting a mix of strong emotions, but mostly head-to-toe anxiety. I wasn't sleeping. I wasn't thinking straight.

All conversations returned to their beginning.

Who is she?

We had fought like crazy, so long, so hard, from state to state, town hall to town hall. We had gone from broke and tired to flush and ecstatic. We were humble underdogs who had won so many primaries it was becoming hard to distinguish them. We were jubilant, committed, and in a groove. My dad had shaken so many hands, walked in so many doors, talked to so many people. Miles and miles of people. And suddenly he seemed to be staking this whole thing that meant so much to him on her.

The way she was chosen—in secrecy—and the way she was abruptly tossed at the country, just five days before the convention, had thrown the media into a feeding frenzy. The investigative reporters didn't know where to begin. The press phones rang nonstop, day and night, and suddenly our ragtag Pirate Ship was bulging with new people, new stories, and dozens of unconfirmed rumors. It was like Wac-A-Mole. Just when one had been beaten down, another popped up.

The Palins seemed like nice, regular people. They were low key and traveled light—with small overnight bags of casual clothes, jeans and sweatpants, regular stuff you'd buy at Macy's or JCPenney. They were definitely shell-shocked but holding it together.

The campaign had intended to stun the world with a surprise running mate, and thought this would get the Republican Party fired up. But this strategy seemed wrongheaded to me. I was starting to see that the American public—or the American media, at any rate—likes to be eased into things. Human beings like routine, predictability, and being able to have expectations about how things will go. Brash, fast, unexpected news is not comforting—or comfortable. From what I could tell, the Obama campaign had mastered the "easing effect." We had not.

Also, I believe if Sarah Palin and her family had been given more time to get to know the campaign, and us, there would have been more trust in our overall organization. Sarah hadn't seen us when we were down and out, before the primaries. She hadn't seen how far we'd come, or the beauty of our struggle. She had no idea of where we had been—or even what we were about. All she knew was our big, polished machine—big planes and big stress—and our bullying campaign manager, Steve Schmidt.

With less secrecy, and more time to get to know each other, there would have been more loyalty and cohesiveness. But, instead, from the minute Sarah arrived the campaign began splitting apart. And rather than joining us, and our campaign, she seemed only to begin her own.

And the media drama that ensued, immediately, began to stir up doubts and fear within our ranks. Uncertainty has a way of doing that. Within two days of the announcement, I had seen a report on an Internet gossip site that Sarah Palin's daughter Bristol was pregnant. This had to be false, I figured, just like the rumor that Sarah Palin's infant son, Trig, wasn't her baby.

But then I remembered how Bristol had stood so quietly, so timidly, at her mother's announcement at that Ohio high school. She was covering her stomach with a big blanket . . . I couldn't stop thinking about it.

WE WERE ON THE BUS TOGETHER IN OHIO, THE DAY after the announcement. Even in the sweltering heat and humidity, Bristol was wearing a big sweatshirt, which I thought was weird. She was aloof, or very shy. Maybe she was just freaked out by her mom's announcement, I thought. Freaked out by suddenly being in the national spotlight, and seeing the clusters of cameras wherever she went. I had had lots of preparation for the strange cardboard existence of daughter-of. But why was she wearing a sweatshirt?

Somewhere in Ohio, I got off the bus and found Brooke Buchanan, who was doing press for the campaign. Brooke was smoking—she was a chain smoker during the campaign—and I entered her cloud of tobacco smoke, close enough to come right out and ask her if the rumors were true that Bristol was pregnant.

Brooke moved her head up and down. Her eyes were covered by her giant Oliver Peoples sunglasses. She was exhaling smoke and just kept nodding.

"What are we going to do?" I asked.

"We're dealing with it."

"How?"

Brooke looked so stressed out. She isn't much older than I but, unlike me, is steady and solid and totally unflappable. Nothing rocked

Brooke—normally. But that day, she looked ragged and overwhelmed. And this scared me.

In politics, you are supposed to take pride in having things under control, tested to perfection, and managed. Every location where you campaign is supposed to be scouted, and studied, ahead of time. Not just for security reasons. You don't want surprises. Surprises are your enemy. And *situations.* That's why remarks are prepared ahead of time, schedules are followed. Control is key. And above all, never look rattled or confused or uncertain.

But this was a *situation* of epic proportions. How would the campaign handle it? How would Sarah Palin? And more than I worried about my dad or the outcome of his campaign, I wondered how it could possibly be okay—in any interpretation of that word—to put a seventeen-year-old girl who had accidentally gotten pregnant in such an awful, public position.

I got back on the bus and stole a look at Bristol. She was sitting in her seat, sweating in her sweatshirt, just staring into space.

Miraculously, she was keeping it together. But she had to be dying inside. I knew what seventeen was like. My little sister, Bridget, was exactly that age. And here Bristol was, the poor girl, I thought—having to cope with the media, the rumors, and all these weirded-out campaign strangers like me, who were now staring at her, and whispering. Oh, eventually we'd all be nice. Of course we would. And the campaign would protect her. But people were going be cruel. I knew they would.

What a world politics is. What an awful world sometimes.

MY BIGGEST FEAR IN LIFE, WHEN I WAS A TEENAGER, was getting pregnant. When I was fourteen, a reporter had asked my father what he would do if I got pregnant and wasn't married. He famously answered, "That would be her decision." This comment had created a mild media storm. I was just fourteen and hadn't had sex, but suddenly I was in the news as a daughter-of in a terrible hypothetical situation. That hypothetical had become my nightmare.

I don't think abstinence until marriage is realistic these days. For one thing, it could drive you into getting married too young—or drive you into marrying somebody with whom you had no physical chemistry. Why would you marry somebody that you hadn't had sex with? Isn't sex monumentally important to a relationship? Why would you keep it a big mystery until the wedding night—when it was too late?

Abstinence doesn't seem practical to me. It seems like a way of avoiding reality and real conversations about complicated things like pregnancy and STDs. Abstinence sends a message that sex is wrong or dirty. It isn't wrong or dirty to me. Also, these vows are usually ineffective—studies have shown that more than half of the young people who take a vow of abstinence until marriage don't keep it, and go on to break it within a year. This heat-of-the-moment change of heart often happens when no contraception is being used.

I am as passionately pro-life as you can imagine. And because of that, I am as passionately pro-contraception as you can imagine too. This is the part of the equation that I don't think conservatives have addressed enough. In fact, it seems completely missing from the sermon they are preaching. They go on and on about how evil and wrong abortion is, but don't like to talk about how easy it is to *not* get pregnant.

Bristol was the newest and most unprepared daughter-of that I had ever seen. And she was literally living my worst nightmare.

The campaign was "dealing with it," according to Brooke. But how? And what on earth did Steve Schmidt have to say? He was so tough and unemotional. Boy, I had messed up plenty on the campaign, and Steve Schmidt had been hard on me, and demanding. Would this news affect how the country accepted Sarah Palin?

"What are you going to do?" I asked Steve, a couple days later.

He shrugged. It was all taken care of.

"People will relate to her more," he said.

This is the essential job of a daughter-of. We are there to make the candidate more human. But in this instance, the price seemed kind of steep.

13

I LOVE MY MOM AND HERE SHE IS

WITHIN JUST A COUPLE DAYS, BRISTOL PALIN'S SWEATSHIRT WAS GONE—REPLACED BY A STUNNING WARDROBE. SHE LOOKED FRESH and beautiful, if not downright angelic. The campaign had announced that she was pregnant a couple days before the convention started, causing a sensation almost as big as Hurricane Gustav, which had lost steam as soon as it hit land.

The campaign had done its job "dealing with it" all right. Rather than an uncomfortable subject to talk about, Bristol was being heralded as a pro-life role model.

I found this troubling. And I thought about my sister, Bridget, and how many conversations she and my mom and I had had about teen pregnancy and the importance of waiting until you were older to have sex. While I admired anyone who didn't try to make an unwanted pregnancy disappear privately with an abortion, I couldn't help but feel a very important message was missing.

Rather than seizing an opportunity to discuss the importance of contraception, the campaign seemed to be glamorizing teen pregnancy.

And rather than a sense of remorse about Bristol's situation, there seemed only glee and excitement. Did the campaign really want to suggest that a pro-life message was more important than a message of how to avoid teenage pregnancy to begin with?

But I kept those thoughts to myself, or mostly to myself, and kept cheerleading myself to go along, be quiet, and mind my own business.

CONVENTION PROTOCOL DICTATES THAT THE NOMINEE arrives after the show has started. When my dad flew into Minneapolis, the campaign notified my family that we were supposed to assemble and greet him on the tarmac. Like everybody else, I wasn't sure what the purpose of this "event" was, aside from a kind of symbolic welcome. But dutifully, I went along and was loaded into a bus, along with my mom and brothers and Bridget. I was wearing leggings, a wrinkled gray dress, and a pair of flats. My hair wasn't brushed and I had very little makeup on. I figured it was a crowd shot, at the very most, and it wouldn't matter what I looked like.

But I was wrong about that. As soon as we got off the bus, I noticed white TV trucks with satellite dishes. There was a giant flatbed truck parked on the tarmac and a riser crowded with what looked like one hundred photographers and cameras.

Uh-oh. This wasn't just a photo op. It was a mega op.

What was going on?

On the tarmac, the Palins gathered too. But unlike my family, who looked a little mismatched, and our clothes barely pulled together, the Palins were stunning, gorgeous, and color-coordinated. They are a spectacularly beautiful family to begin with, no matter what they are wearing—and perhaps even better looking in person than on TV. Now they shined with movie star perfection. Their hair had been cut and styled. Their makeup was professionally done. Their clothes were amazing. All together, they looked so wholesome and all-American, it was dazzling. "They look like a J.Crew ad," Heather said.

"Yeah," my brother Jack said, "and we look like crap."

I couldn't help but zero in on Levi Johnston, Bristol Palin's boyfriend at the time, who was almost unrecognizable from the guy who'd appeared two days before. The transformation was incredible.

My father got off the plane, waved, and came down the steps. He walked over immediately to embrace Bristol and Levi.

Huh? The whole thing seemed off, like he had traveled here to bless their union—and their unborn child. I told myself it was just one of those unfortunate but necessary fake moments that can happen on a campaign—but which I hated and my dad usually managed to avoid. How had we wound up here? I longed for a simpler scene and a simpler running mate, a straight-ahead and experienced politician like good old Joe Lieberman, who always kept it real and didn't make himself the center of dramas or chaos.

But here we were instead, putting out forest fires, contorting ourselves to make everything seem fine, and trying too hard to not show how scared we were.

The Palins were nice and down-to-earth. I've said that before. And I mean no disrespect to them when I say this, but when they arrived from Alaska and unpacked their bags, they brought dramas, stress, complications, panic, and loads of uncertainty. And they brought a tabloid-attention-getting quality that my family has never had—and, God willing, never will.

For my father's embrace of Bristol and Levi, the cameras began clicking and recording. The media heat of the moment was palpable. We were all photographed, again and again, and within hours, we would all be splattered across the Internet.

Great, I thought, looking down at my lamentable outfit. One more bad photograph of me at a convention that will live on forever. There were so many of those. So many, I was almost used to it.

★

HAPPILY, THERE ARE NO PICTURES OF ME AT MY FIRST Republican convention, when my mom and dad were delegates for Reagan in 1984. That's because I was in utero. In 1996, when I was in fifth grade, the convention was in San Diego and Senator Bob Dole was nominated. My brothers and I made hokey homemade glitter signs that said, "We love you, Dad," and stuff like that on them. It is against the rules to bring a homemade sign into a convention—that's why all the signs you see on TV are so uniform, a way to communicate order and control—so when we stood on chairs and waved our unique signs, a swarm of reporters came over to interview me, because I was the oldest kid.

That year produced lots of hideous photos that still make me cringe, and sometimes when I'm having an overblown fantasy of fame, I imagine that they will be used to shame me and destroy all chances of me being thought of as a cool person. I wore an American flag dress to that convention. Yep. But it wasn't the only one, either. For years, my mother dressed me in a wardrobe of embarrassing all-American outfits. She had a weakness for anything with stars and stripes or red, white, and blue.

Four years later, at the convention in 2000, I was about to start high school and was feeling very grown-up. I remember having a really great time in Philadelphia. My dad was still sort of the wild card of the GOP in those days and I was aware of that on some level, and loved it. I got to sit and watch him give a beautiful speech on the convention stage. Our family was placed in one of those "family boxes" in the front row of the balcony, so the TV cameras can record every single facial expression.

It's really like sitting in a cage. While you are looking at the stage, the cameras are looking at you. The nice thing is that it doesn't last long. The family box is only for the family of the person giving the speech. So as soon as Dad was done, and the clapping had died down, we had to evacuate the box so that the next family could sit there.

Something like musical chairs, I guess. Cameras don't move. The families do. The only thing that matters is that you keep your face from registering any emotion while it's happening. My mom is incredible at this, and sphinx-like. Her face rarely flickers with emotion in a public setting. But I can always look in her eyes and see what's really going on.

My other vivid memory of the 2000 convention is seeing a giant effigy of a penis with George Bush's face on top of it, just beyond the convention center barriers. I was really confused. Was it supposed to be a penis or was it George Bush?

I had never seen a really distasteful political protest before. And I couldn't understand why people hated Republicans so much. This was before George W. Bush was elected—before the Florida recount, 9/11, Iraq, Katrina, or anything else you want to blame the Bush administration for—and yet, even then, there was vitriol. Such anger.

No one would ever feel that way about my dad, right? I remember thinking that he was much more special than most politicians, and more beloved. But of course I was wrong about that. Extremists like to protest and they don't seem to care about subtleties or distinctions. The world is only black and white to them. This is true of the Left as well as the Right. The enemy is the enemy to them, no matter what. And whoever that enemy is, they just can't be human.

AFTER ALL THOSE MOMENTS OF STANDING SILENTLY AT conventions in the past, of looking perfect and doing my little wave to the crowd and flashing a smile, it was unimaginable to me that someday I might be able to open my mouth and actually say something. To be animated and alive! To be allowed a voice!

Most of all, I was really excited about introducing my mother. At the Democratic convention, Chelsea Clinton had introduced her mother and I had paid close attention to what an excellent job she did. Chelsea was so poised and almost spookily calm. In my head, I imagined just how I'd be—and what I'd say. My mom was really excited too.

But whenever I raised the subject with the Groomsmen, I could not get any traction—or even schedule a meeting to discuss it. It was so frustrating. I had done my part and seen the image consultant. I'd cut off my long hair. My clothes were toned down. I'd even tried very hard to prevent so many *likes* from falling from my tongue.

Whenever I asked about it, nobody had an answer.

The convention was not about me. I knew that. But when you are twenty-three years old everything seems about you, despite all evidence to the contrary. And as much as I tried to keep my focus and remember that the real goal was to get my dad elected, I kept becoming distracted by my own issues and concerns.

Was I introducing Mom or not?

Was I?

The days passed and nothing was said about it. Eventually too much time passed—and obviously a decision had been made against it. When I pressed, there were all kinds of explanations that might have been true, but at the time, I didn't buy for one second. Like "There isn't enough time to prepare."

Or "Nobody can think of something for you to say."

So lame.

It didn't seem complicated to me. "I know what to say," I told them. "Hello, my name is Meghan McCain. I love my mom and here she is!"

My convention speech was quickly becoming just another bad bargain that I made with the campaign. When I complained to one of my dad's advisers, he said, "You are lucky to even be here at all."

Really? Was that true?

14

THE DIVA WHO FELL TO EARTH

I T WAS BEGINNING TO DAWN ON ME THAT I WASN'T QUITE AS VALUED ON THE CAMPAIGN AS I HAD PRE-VIOUSLY THOUGHT. LOOKING BACK, I REALIZED that it had been going on for a while, and showed itself in the way people treated me, how they danced around certain subjects, and tip-toed, timidly. Nobody was being real or direct with me. Instead, they were vague and spoke in super-calm voices, like Nurse Ratched in *One Flew Over the Cuckoo's Nest.*

They didn't feel lucky to have me. No. In the eyes of the campaign, I was like a curse, a brat, a diva, a monstrous daughter-of. Or maybe I'm giving myself too much credit again. I was a small and pretty un-important detail, in the vast scheme of things. All I needed to do was keep my mouth shut.

In the beginning, when I first joined, there were only a small number of us—we called ourselves "the Originals"—and it felt like a family. In places like New Hampshire, I felt safe and wasn't particu-larly careful about everything I said. The rule that I live by—*there are no secrets*—worked for me in that environment. But not anymore.

Now I annoyed people. I know that. Just being young, and acting young, can be super-irritating to older people. I was the daughter of the candidate, too, and this added to the sense of entitlement that people seemed to suspect I was carrying around. But this is *not* how I have ever thought of myself. My brothers and sister and I were all raised to be real, and pull our own freight, and not walk around expecting the world to wait on us. My two brothers are both in the military. I don't think it gets more un-entitled than that.

The last thing I wanted to do was call my parents and whine. They had enough on their plate as it was. What was I going to say, *Hey, I know you are running for president, but so-and-so forgot to invite me to that reception . . .*

Forgot to put me on the list . . .

Forgot to tell me where to go . . .

I felt lost in the shuffle. But, like I said, in the scheme of things, my complaints were small potatoes and so was I. What bothered me most was that, underneath all the drama, I felt a separation building between me and the rest of the campaign, which had been my home since graduating from college. And worse, I felt a separation growing between me and my parents. With each passing day, it was becoming a bigger hassle to get past security just to see them.

NO MATTER WHO YOU ARE, OR WHERE YOU COME FROM, you had to think that Sarah Palin's lipstick on a pit bull speech was incredible. There was so much tension building beforehand—everybody wondering whether she would choke, how she would look, whether she could pull it off. I don't think anybody on the campaign was relaxed about it. And it seemed to make matters more stressful that very few people had met her, or even seen her. Almost as soon as she was announced, she had gone underground to prepare her remarks.

And when she delivered her speech with such confidence, so naturally, as if she had given millions of convention speeches already, even ad-libbing some jokes, the sense of excitement in the hall was palpable.

In the family box in front of the TV cameras, the Palins were assembled, looking inhumanly gorgeous and well groomed. The media frenzy around them was astonishing—they were rock stars, from Bristol and Levi down to little Trig.

I wish I could have been a better sport about the fact that Sarah and her family now seemed to dominate the entire convention. Everyone was so excited by the Palins' newness and real-life dramas, their exotic Alaskan lifestyle and their cohesiveness. The campaign's focus, as well as the world's, was suddenly completely on them. But it was starting to seem like reality TV to me. I kept wondering, *why are these people taking over our lives?*

Later that night, I happened to be sitting in the hotel lobby bar with Shannon and Heather when Sarah walked by—and the campaign staff and journalists in the room exploded in spontaneous applause, and then charged at her. A rope line formed, almost magically, as people began waiting their turn to talk to her, ask for an autograph, or to have their picture taken with her. I mean, even journalists were waiting to be photographed with her.

Sarah was basking in a kind of golden haze of glory—and who could blame her? She was not just an overnight success or even a political Cinderella story. She was a sudden, freakishly huge, full-fledged phenomenon. It seemed too much. And it seemed too easy. From my chair across the way, I watched with incredulity. I had never seen anything like it, ever, even in all my travels with Dad.

Maybe there was a chip on my shoulder or maybe I was jealous. It was hard to collect all the complicated feelings I had. But earlier that day, it had been made painfully clear to me how low I'd sunk, in terms of status on the campaign.

I had wandered down the hallway outside my room at the convention hotel, where I was staying on the same floor as my parents, my brothers and sister, as well as senior staff. My hair was wet and my face was bare. I was heading to the "makeup room" in the middle of our floor, where two hairdressers and two makeup artists had been installed to glam up everybody. And I mean *everybody*. There was nothing more important, suddenly, than how we looked.

The scheduling of these miraculous makeovers was really crazy, and stressful. We all needed to look perfect and camera-ready when we needed to be, but quite often there weren't enough stylists to accommodate all of us—my parents, both Sarah and Todd Palin, and our families.

I was running late that morning, and hoping to get some help with my hair for a photo shoot. I entered the makeup room and looked around. But all the chairs were taken. The stylists were busy with the Palin kids, as well as Levi.

"Can you make time for me?" I asked.

"You'll have to wait," the makeup artist replied. Levi, Bristol, Willow, and Piper, who was seven, needed to be styled first.

The makeup artist shook her head slowly, always the sign of a power trip going on. "They'll be getting more airtime."

Silence fell over the room. It was so quiet you could hear the sound of the reality check going on inside my head. I tried really hard to call upon Meggie Mac, my alter ego, the perfect, polite, and smiling daughter-of. But she failed to appear.

There was only one thing left to do: Go back to my room and do my hair and makeup myself.

The Palins had taken the lead now. The makeup artist was right. I should have thanked her for making me take that big red pill. All my delusions of having an impact, or the importance of my fan base and the unique hits on my blog, vanished like the steam rising from my hair dryer.

I was irrelevant. And in fact, I might have never been relevant to begin with—even way back in Mount Pleasant, Iowa, when we only had one damn bus.

I felt a joke in the air, but it was on me.

MY DAD WAS THE LAST TO SPEAK. IT IS A BEAUTIFUL tradition of a political convention, when the nominee finally appears in front of the jubilant hall and accepts the nomination. Seeing Dad come onstage and make his acceptance speech was one of the top five best moments of my life. I was entranced by him, and uplifted. His voice and strength grounded me, as they always do. Then I started to cry.

I was in the family box—that place where you aren't supposed to show anything except a kind of mesmerized stare—and tried to fight it, and fight it. But my mind began to play back moments from the past year, our days in Iowa and New Hampshire, and all that the campaign had been through, the road trips and dustups, the intrigues and hilarity. I thought about my dad and all that he'd been through—as a boy, as a soldier, a senator, a dad, a candidate running for president. He'd tried so hard, and given so much. And here he was, accepting the burden and honor and great responsibility of representing the Republican Party in the coming election.

I looked around the great hall. It seemed like the biggest room I'd ever sat in. It was humbling, and real. All these people had gathered, all this hope and energy, because of what my father had done and who he is. And what he represents. My dad was what I believed in. He was what I had signed on for. His commitment to change, and to making the country a better place, was daunting and inspiring and made me feel so good. I cried harder and tried to muffle the crying sounds coming out of my mouth. Little mouse squeaks came out instead.

It was true, I saw that now. *I was lucky to be there at all.*

15

A BUS OF MY OWN

WITH THE CONVENTION OVER I EXPECTED
THINGS TO DIE DOWN—AND GET MORE RE-
LAXED. I KEPT WAITING TO FEEL BETTER,
and more grounded. It never happened.

The campaign shifted gears all right. Everything sped up and became more intense. Maybe the transition from the primary season, to
loopy convention chaos, to general election mode seemed gradual to
some people. But for me, our entire world had ramped up and hyped
up, almost overnight.

New Hampshire was a faraway dream, a beautiful memory that
was fading in the nonstop noise of now.

But there was no going back. Only forward. But forward was a
place of insomnia and anxiety. The tension at headquarters was in evidence everywhere—in the voices of staffers, in the tone of e-mails and
orders, in the way decisions got made. Nothing was ever calm or
quiet.

Unless you had been acclimating yourself to this kind of environment over the preceding months, I'm sure it would have seemed

impossible to survive it at all—like being thrown in a room where, instead of music blaring, it was the sound of an extended scream.

I spent a couple weeks in New York and Los Angeles, doing a few campaign events with my parents and going on TV to talk about a children's book that I had written, *My Dad, John McCain*. I was so nervous beforehand, I couldn't sleep or eat. It was such a big deal to me. I went overboard and wore the most conservative suits too. The journalists were all pretty sweet, and treated me with kid gloves. In the end, the campaign was surprised I survived it. I made some mistakes on TV—bumbled a few lines—but nothing as dramatic as the mistakes the campaign thought I'd make. The campaign's biggest fear, I later learned, was that I'd say the F-word on morning TV.

Looking back now, I can see that after the convention I was worn down and running on fumes. I'm sure you know how it is—I can't be the only person who gets cranky and negative when she's tired and stressed out. Wherever I looked, I saw problems and irritations and people I didn't like. The campaign became the focus of my animosity.

Sometimes I believed that Steve Schmidt was making me nuts. Then I would think about the Bus Nazi and Blond Amazon, and so many other campaign staffers who drove me nuts, and I had to admit that the entire campaign was getting to me. The problem was, I had seen too much, and I knew too much. After fourteen months on the road, familiarity had truly bred contempt. At one low point, I remember wishing that, once the election was over, I would never see any of these people again.

Luckily, I never stay in a bad mood for long. Sometimes all I have to do is remember to be grateful for being alive and healthy, and for all the opportunities I've been given. I remember the people I love and the causes that I care about. There was so much more in life to be thankful for than to complain about. But after the convention, when I tried my tricks for adjusting my attitude, I found it wasn't so easy.

You know the expression "Now is the winter of our discontent" from Shakespeare's *Richard III*? Well, my winter came a few months early, like the middle of September. I just couldn't shake it.

It's not like I had an enemies list or anything. It wasn't individuals so much as *types* that bugged me. And while I hate being put in a box myself, or categorized as a *type*, I have to recognize how difficult it is to not do it to others.

Political fleas were one type that bugged me. These were staffers who had jumped off the dead dogs like Giuliani and Romney and hopped on my dad at the last minute. Maybe fleas is too negative—it sounds like they were feeding off my dad and sucking his blood. The relationship is obviously more symbiotic. Amoebas might be better. It was like a bunch of foreign amoebas from different campaigns joined ours and suddenly we were a much bigger amoeba ourselves.

A lot of the new amoebas were former Bush White House people, too. This troubled me a lot more than it seemed to trouble anybody else. Let's face it. That administration didn't have its act together.

Most of all, the résumé-polishing flea/amoebas bugged me. They showed up to add a line to their résumés and didn't really care about my dad. Loyalty was foreign to them, because everything was just about their own career enhancement. One guy on our campaign, who bragged endlessly about his MIT degree, told me two days before the election that my dad had a 30 percent chance of winning. I wanted to deck him. It turned out Mr. MIT had been sending his résumé around for a month already, looking for a job. His lack of integrity was really stunning and I wish he could be driven from politics. But there's no chance of that. All of this will be forgotten in 2012, when he joins up to work for the next Republican nominee. And trust me, he'll wait until the last minute to jump on board. He doesn't want too many losers to foul his résumé.

As far as the media was concerned, even at this point, my father was looking like the man *not* to watch. Maybe from a campaign's perspective, there is no such thing as balanced, satisfying coverage. But you didn't have to read too closely between the lines to assume that the entire country was in an Obama-loving craze, even when the polls showed that the race was close.

I was done with the media, in any case, and just as sick of the political beat reporters as I was of our campaign staff. The behavior of many campaign staffers and advisers and reporters during the final months of the campaign appalled me. *These people were grown-ups?* And this is what a presidential campaign looks like?

AS IT TURNS OUT, EVERYBODY WAS SICK OF ME, TOO. IF you thought my basic popularity levels couldn't sink any lower than during the convention, guess again. Almost as soon as the general election process ramped up, I couldn't do anything right.

Everywhere I turned, and for everything I did, I was either ignored or berated for bad behavior. At the back of the Third Bus, where Mr. Burns the Bus Nazi always put me by now, if Shannon and Heather and I danced to music or got slaphappy and laughed too much, people were appalled.

Suddenly it was a huge crime if I gave random people—volunteers and fans we'd meet on the road—tours of the Straight Talk Express. I loved showing people what the buses looked like inside, giving them a peek at history, and watching them light up in huge smiles. But I was told, point blank, to stop.

My swearing was the final straw. I tried to stop—I really did—but in high stress situations, the F-bombs would just launch out of me like hiccups. When word got back to my parents about it, they were embarrassed and called to talk to me about it. I felt so bad, and problematic.

Word went out that we weren't supposed to swear in front of the Palins, or at least, all the little Palins. But I never did, anyway. But at the same time, I had to wonder why there was a seven-year-old girl riding on a campaign bus, whether staff were swearing around her or not. Piper is an adorable daughter-of, as well as being a sweet girl, but

I didn't get how traveling on a campaign bus in pivotal moments of a national election was good for her or good for the campaign.

I was raised very differently. My mom and dad have strong feelings about not exposing their kids to the nitty-gritty world of campaigning—or even politics. Bridget was seventeen and my parents were both pretty protective of her. When asked why he kept his family out of the limelight, Dad always said that he wanted us to be independent and have our own lives. He never wanted to look like he was using us to warm hearts or gain some kind of emotional advantage.

We were never urged to join Dad on the campaign trail. He seemed content that his oldest three kids, my half brothers and half sister from his first marriage, lived full lives of their own and had no interest in whistle-stops and waving on stage. When I made it known that I wanted to join the campaign as a twenty-two-year-old college graduate, I had to convince my dad's advisers, not just my parents, that I was planning to contribute, be responsible for myself, and not get in the way. If I didn't toe the line and cooperate, my dad had no plans to bail me out.

Clearly, the Palins didn't see things the same way. Maybe I'm not being sympathetic enough to working moms, or to little Piper, who seemed to enjoy wandering to the back of the bus or plane to butter up the media. Sarah Palin was the campaign's secret weapon—on the surface, anyway. Supporters were going nuts for her, and Middle America, and far Right donors, too. Women appeared to be almost obsessed with her—thousands of them, cheering and even crying at her events. Record-breaking crowds turned out for her events; it was amazing and beautiful. We finally had Obama-sized appeal.

Dad was thrilled with her—and appreciated what she could do, and all the attention and energy that she brought to the campaign. He told his advisers that he loved doing events with her—"We're so much better together than we are apart!"—but the Groomsmen convinced him that it made more sense to split them up. That way, they could cover twice as much ground, and do twice as many events, in a day.

The media was falling for her too. Sarah was a beauty, seemed kind of groovy, and had sex appeal, too. Ratings went up when she came onscreen. But my father's advisers, as happy as they were by the excitement over their VP pick, were a little spooked by the fascination and popularity that Sarah drew to her. The big gamble they'd made by choosing her was causing a whole lot of stress. I called her "the Time Bomb." I was waiting for her to explode. There was a fine line between genius and insanity, they say, and choosing her as the running mate was starting to seem like the definition of that line.

The brighter the spotlight, the more difficult a mistake would be to handle. Dad's advisers wanted Sarah to look prepared and worldly—and from what I could tell, there was a massive effort to outfit and educate her. I sympathized with how difficult she must have found this Pygmalion process, and dealing with Steve Schmidt—ugh—couldn't have been fun. He didn't seem to have a gentle side or a soft touch.

I had never felt comfortable complaining about Steve to my parents. I'm sure Sarah didn't either.

I'D BEEN IN CALIFORNIA FOR A WEEK WITH MY BLOG staff when the campaign finally made its mind up about me: Don't come back. I was a distraction, too controversial, and not playing well with others. The blog could go away too, for all they cared. It just caused complaints. My personal stock had sunk so low, staffers didn't want their pictures on it anymore.

I was given a choice. It wasn't a nice one, either.

I could quit and go home or else I would be effectively banished to the heartland on an extended tour of regional McCain campaign headquarters for five weeks. It didn't take a genius to do the simple arithmetic: They wanted me out of their hair until a few days before the election, when they would trot me out again, like a circus animal in a suit. Stand. Wave. Smile.

The irony wasn't lost on me. Here I'd been ruminating about how

SEXY POLITICS

the Palins weren't "ready for prime time" when, in fact, it was me all along. I was such a prodigal daughter-of that nobody wanted me around.

Home.

It was starting to sound pretty nice.

Home.

I could barely imagine it.

No more tyranny from the Groomsmen. No more seating assignments from the Bus Nazi. No more having to watch the antics of the media circus and its gaga behavior over the Obamas and strange lust for the Palins.

I could live in my jammies and UGG boots, watch TV and YouTube videos all day, and eat healthy food. I could go for days without worrying about my hair, or even washing it. What if I stopped brushing it altogether?

I would be free to be me, say whatever, and drop F-bombs all over the house. I could swim in the pool, pork out on Mexican food, and hang with my Scottsdale girlfriends who didn't care about politics.

Or, I could have my own bus.

Are you serious?

My own bus for six weeks? And it was going to be one of the nice buses with comfy seats and clean upholstery, a new bathroom where there weren't cigarette burns on the toilet seat, and AC that didn't blow out pure mold.

I could fill the mini-fridge with Diet Pepsi and Starbucks frappuccinos. I could fill the drawers and cabinets with M&M's and Luna Bars, Swedish fish and Doritos.

I could lead as many tours of the bus as I wanted, play any music I liked, sing as loudly as possible, and express myself as colorfully as I could—even if every other word would have been inappropriate for Piper.

The road was calling.

And I answered.

16

HOW I STARTED FAKING IT

I'M NOT GOING TO LIE AND SAY THAT I WASN'T IN-CREDIBLY HURT WHEN THE CAMPAIGN FIRED ME. I KEPT COMING UP WITH WORDS FOR WHAT HAD HAP-pened, and trying to find a way to accept it. Was it a promotion or a demotion? Was I fired—or just *excused*? What should I say on the blog?

Heather came up with a brilliant idea right away. It was time for niceness, good cheer, bubbly behavior. A Little Miss Sunshine strategy.

"Don't let anybody see that you're upset," Heather said. "We're all going to act like we're having the time of our lives."

"What?"

"Fake it 'til you make it."

Usually I don't go in for strategies, but in this case, I decided to follow Heather's advice. On the blog, I was upbeat and cheery about ventur-ing out on my own. In photographs, I am smiling and laughing—happily meeting and greeting people.

All the effort that had gone into the blog, and reaching out to young voters and moderates like me, seemed to have added up to nothing. I had tried so hard, and cared so much about every tiny detail. But now, faced with Obama, a pop culture icon who had Jay-Z on his iPod, our campaign pretty much gave up on the youth vote. There was no point chasing it. Moderates had fallen for him too. So we were sticking to the old Bush strategy from 2000 and 2004 and honing in on the dependable Republican base—old people and the right-wing.

It was like a game of poker. You had to play your hand. But looking ahead, at 2012 and 2016, I wondered what would happen to the party when the old people died off and the base consisted entirely of the Christian Right. Evangelicals are a well-organized group, and I have to admire their passion and resilience. But this country was founded on religious freedom, not religious constraints.

My mom was amazing during this time. She called, and kept in touch, and was supportive in every possible way. "You are going to be great on the road," she kept saying. "You're a natural." I would have felt impossibly bad, I think, without her love and encouragement. Sometimes you still need your mom to tell you everything's going to be okay. The ground under my feet was solid. I had to keep remembering that.

"Just be grateful for everything you have," she said. "And don't dwell on the things you don't."

So I kept it together and tried to be super-appreciative when Claire Merkel at campaign headquarters began designing a bus tour of the heartland for me. The basic concept was that I would meet supporters and voters in Pennsylvania, Ohio, Colorado, and Florida—key swing states in the general election. Claire was lining up biker rallies, receptions with state party chairmen, and visits to college campuses. I would have to give speeches, autograph books, address crowds, and give pep talks—the sort of campaigning that I had never done.

Shannon, Heather, and I would continue the blog, chronicling our days on the road with posts and pictures—as though nothing had happened. Would any of our readers really notice that I wasn't on the main campaign, following my dad around, or care?

I felt better when I heard Melissa Shuffield would be coming along to do press and scheduling, and Frank LaRose—a former Green Beret and fantastic guy—would be doing advance. Best of all, we'd have the most incredible driver, Jay Frye, whenever my dad didn't need him. With the campaign's permission, I convinced Josh Rupley, an amazing hairstylist in LA, to leave his salon and keep me looking good until election day. Josh is always upbeat and has the most sincere self-deprecating humor, which made me belly-laugh. He was just what I needed in the trenches.

I fantasized about that day in the future, after November, when I would never brush my hair again. But until then, there was no doubt that I was supposed to look a certain way or pay the consequences when the blogosphere went wild with cruel remarks—which just caused more headaches for the campaign. I was determined to be a help now, not a distraction.

Being your own person was honorable. But being a member of a team—and being willing to tone yourself down, play nice, and fit in—was part of politics and public life. Looking back on my year-plus on the campaign, this had been my biggest struggle. I didn't fit in easily, and part of me didn't want to. I may be passionately pro-life, and in favor of a strong defense and the war in Iraq, but there were all kinds of things about me that rattled the stereotype. But somehow, the party wanted everything black or white. And I was gray.

Even my education, which I was so proud of, had been ridiculed on the campaign for being "Ivy League," words that the campaign now used to brand Obama as an "elitist." My dad had started making cracks about my alma mater, Columbia, in his stump speech. It was a running joke that I'd gone to a "socialist" school and had had a "ridiculous major" like art history.

I knew my dad was only kidding. He was proud of me—and had my graduation picture on the main wallpaper of his cellphone. I think if I ever told him that the jokes about Columbia bothered me, he would have stopped. But I thought, hey, go ahead and make a joke out of me if it helps. I will take one for the team—no big deal. But when it ended up being a joke *everywhere,* I started getting self-conscious. I heard it on the bus and the plane and even among the press corps. *Here comes the art history major. Ha, ha.*

"She went to Columbia, where the President of Iran just spoke. Can you believe that?"

"How did you do it, Meghan?"

Why did I have to fit into a tidy little box of a person, just to become acceptable to the Republican Party? Why did anybody? Why couldn't an individual—with her own unique tastes and proclivities, philosophy and leanings—be accepted? And how come if you went to one of the most demanding schools in the country, it meant that you were a socialist? I knew how much my generation delighted in its freedoms and disliked being boxed in. My college friends were proud of how hard they'd worked to get into Columbia and of the education they'd gotten there. Why would a political party want to turn off all these smart people with demands that didn't matter? More importantly, how could it win elections?

And why were the young doomed to become Democrats just because they weren't accepted elsewhere?

ONE OF OUR FIRST EVENTS IN OHIO WAS A BIKER RALLY. Have you ever spent a day around hundreds of spirited bikers? The feeling in the air was so free, and fun, and vibrant, the main campaign seemed like a distant memory.

Ohio was a beautiful state for cruising around in our bus. We sped through rolling green hills and spectacular farmland. Along the way, the people we met were friendly and down-to-earth and the small towns were vibrant and innocent.

I fell in love with Columbus, a gorgeous city. I heard it called "the San Francisco of the Midwest," because of its large gay population— and it was there that I met for the first time with a group of Log Cabin

Republicans. If there was ever a talented, committed slice of America that was eager to play an active role in politics, and the Republican Party, but didn't feel accepted or wanted, they were it. My gripes about not fitting in felt pretty pathetic by comparison.

We discussed gay marriage—it was my first serious conversation about this issue—and why the party of limitless freedom, self-reliance, and the individual couldn't wrap its mind around supporting it. This one meeting sparked a passion in me that continues today. I regard marriage equality as this generation's civil rights call to arms. How can we claim this country is truly free when there are still citizens who are separate and not equal?

With each event and new day, campaigning on my own became a little easier. I enjoyed seeing new faces and having direct contact with supporters. They were so much happier than the campaign staff!! And maybe it helped that I had watched my father do "meet and greets" my entire life. He loved them so much—and made it look like such fun. When I gave my first speech, I was so nervous, though—on the verge of meltdown. But I did okay, thanks to lots of coaching from Shannon, Heather, and Melissa.

More than anything, I started to look forward to visiting the offices of McCain volunteers. They believed to their very core in what we were doing and were so happy to meet me. I think it made them feel more connected to my dad. Taking them on a tour of the inside of our bus was the most fun of all. It seemed like such a small thing, letting somebody see part of the Straight Talk Express, where my dad had spent so much time in the last year. People would freak out and go crazy because it was a little piece of the election, a little piece of history.

It was a piece of my dad, too, and I saw how much he meant to people by the way they treated me—and the things they said. It's not such a bad thing to be reminded, like that, of how loved your dad is.

Giving a pep talk to an office of volunteers—or even just one person—came naturally to me. My mom was right about that. I always told volunteers that I was so appreciative of them, and of the chance to meet them.

And the more I said it, the more I was.

The following week, in Pennsylvania, I signed books, shook hands, kissed babies. The whole bit. If anybody had told me just a month before that I would enjoy this—or find it easy and natural—I wouldn't have believed them. But it was true.

"You have so much of your dad in you," my mom had said. I was now seeing that—so clearly. It was almost as if his personality had been literally injected into my veins.

17

WHAT'S UP, NASHVILLE?!

THE FIRST PRESIDENTIAL DEBATE IN OXFORD, MISSISSIPPI, HAD BEEN DECLARED A DRAW BY MANY PUNDITS. SO THE SECOND DEBATE IN NASHVILLE, just eleven days later, had a lot riding on it. Polls were also showing a widening gap between my dad and Obama, with my dad trailing by as much as nine points.

I had never believed in polls. We had proved them wrong so many times in the last year. If the polls were right, we wouldn't have won in New Hampshire. But now, with the general election just a month away, it was hard to not be distracted by them. We were really in the final throes of the campaign.

Walking into the auditorium at Belmont University, where the debate was held, I knew instantly that things had changed—and the stakes had gone up. Unlike the hometown and almost intimate feeling of the debates during the primaries, all of which I had attended, the Curb Event Center was crawling with Secret Service agents, campaign staff and advisers, famous members of the press, and everything else that you imagine. It felt like the Olympics or a prizefight.

It was Dad versus Obama. I was excited to see Dad in a town hall–style debate format and I knew he'd do well. But the way the media was spinning it, there wasn't anything my dad could do that was exciting anymore. He was just an old white guy going up against a young handsome superstar, the smartest and coolest man ever to walk the earth.

MY MOM AND I WALKED WITH LINDSEY GRAHAM, ONE of my favorite senators and a close family friend, into the Curb Event Center—where the debate was being held—and made our way through a traffic jam of bodies. I had chosen to wear a pair of way-too-high heels and remember thinking that all I needed to do was make it to my seat without stumbling or falling flat on my face. If I could do that, I'd be happy.

But it was really hard to walk—much less keep up with the flow of bodies. My mom and Lindsey and I passed through an incredibly long hallway and finally pushed our way inside the Curb Center. A few photographers were waiting to take pictures of my mom and me. After a few snaps, they quickly moved on.

Sitting down in my assigned seat, I relaxed, but not for long. The room was freezing—truly, uncomfortably and horribly freezing. Earlier, the campaign advance team had come to inspect the site and returned to report that the venue was especially cold—air-conditioned to the point of refrigerated. A small space heater was put where my mom was sitting, but it didn't quite reach to me.

From my arctic zone, my teeth chattering, I watched the entrance of Michelle Obama into the center. She was swarmed by dozens of photographers—literally swarmed—flashbulbs flashing, paparazzi style.

Nothing like that had happened for Mom, I have to say. It was just a couple polite snaps and the photographers were gone. But the swarm around Michelle Obama became so intense that, eventually, her staff had to shoo the media away.

I know that a polite lie is appropriate here and I should be mature and say that I wasn't bothered by this. But of course I was. The Obamas are mega-stars and had won the beauty contest, clearly, but wasn't the media supposed to appear to be neutral? Isn't some restraint in order? I'm not even sure Michelle Obama was enjoying the fuss.

Seeing Michelle Obama in person for the first time, I couldn't help but notice how striking she is. I had seen her on TV and in photographs. But now, it was painfully obvious that along with being more popular with the media than my mom, she is as tall as a supermodel and her clothes looked incredible.

That's when my mood started to sink.

Great, I remember thinking. Let's get this damn night over with.

Pundits later said that my dad lost. Others said he won. To others, it was a draw. Depending on which network you watched, the outcome was reported differently. It didn't matter how hard these outlets tried, but it seemed impossible for reporters and pundits and TV show producers to keep their personal hopes and dreams inside, and not cloud their impressions.

Did my dad win or lose? I don't really remember what my own judgment was. I just felt exhausted and restless and down. After my idyllic days in the heartland, enjoying the small pleasures of town-to-town campaigning, it was hard to suddenly find myself surrounded by main campaign staffers and honchos, not to mention the Three Groomsmen. Their anxiety seemed infectious.

I was so proud of my dad, and wondered, once again, how he handled the tense atmosphere and stress so amazingly well. He was always assured and strong. Was there anything that fazed him? If only I had inherited that personality trait too.

★

EARLIER IN THE YEAR, WHEN COUNTRY MUSIC LEGEND John Rich and his band came on the road for my dad, Shannon, Heather, and I had made friends with them instantly. They were a lively bunch—unforgettable, really—and their friendship and company became a wonderful break and relief after so many weeks around the stressed-out campaign types. In particular, I had bonded with John's sidekick, Fred Gill, aka "Two Foot Fred," a little person and incredible dynamo who opened John's show. Some people really come into your life at just the right moment. And Fred sure had.

At a time when it felt like no rock star would ever come out in support, John and Fred and the rest of the band not only came on the road for my father, but performed with great enthusiasm and energy. He had even written a song called "Raising McCain," which we used to play at rallies to get people fired up.

I also knew from previous trips to Nashville that it was a fun, warm, welcoming Southern town that was full of Republicans and loaded with fun bars. I'm not the only one who feels this way: There is definitely something unique in the air of Nashville that makes you want to stay out all night, and soak up every second of life.

And after that debate, I needed to soak up something.

That's how my friends and I wound up at The Spot. It was John Rich's private bar overlooking Broadway, the Nashville strip—and exactly as exclusive, crazy, fun, and kitschy as you would imagine a country legend's private bar to be.

"So what did you think of the debate?" I asked John as soon as we sat down with a drink.

"In all honesty," he said, "I thought your father went too easy on Obama."

I appreciated John giving it to me straight. You can always count on him to tell it like it is. This was a common complaint among Republicans, that my father and the campaign were not hitting Obama hard enough, particularly on his ties to Reverend Wright and ACORN. Say what you want, my father chose the classy route. He rises above the fray.

I changed the subject, realizing that I wasn't up to talking shop, particularly if I was going to have to defend my dad. I had another idea, anyway. Hoping that Frank, Shannon, Heather, and I could see more of Nashville—I'd been talking about what a fantastic city it is for the last week—I asked John if he'd take us honky-tonking, Nashville-speak for bar hopping. The tradition was to go from country bar to country bar along the strip, drinking and listening to the most talented group of singers you could ever find in a one-mile radius.

And honky-tonking we did. Wherever we went, John created quite a stir—and the more I drank, the more I loved the stir that we were making. We went to the famous Tootsies, then another bar, and another, finally hitting the last establishment at the end of the strip.

There were a few beers in me. And I had no idea how late it was—or how early in the morning—when I asked John if he'd sing "Raising McCain" to everybody in the bar.

"Only if you introduce me," he said.

I was still scared about speaking in public in those days—to the point of being totally neurotic about it. That bit of "media training" hadn't helped. Instead, it made me worry about every single word (*like*) that came out of my mouth. But I wanted to hear John sing.

Josh and Shannon patted me on the back and somebody—who was it?—poured me a big shot of whiskey. I polished it off in a gulp and ran to the microphone, trying hard not to stumble in my way-too-high heels.

I jumped onstage and then, to everybody's astonishment, I hollered at the top of my lungs, "WHAT'S UP, NASHVILLE?!?!"

The bar roared back.

And when I identified myself by saying that my father was running for president, the room went crazy—an explosion of sound and applause, yelling and cheering. I had never heard such beautiful noise. And in that moment, it didn't matter how glamorous Barack and Michelle Obama were, or what all the pundits in the universe were saying, or how uptight and condescending the Groomsmen were being to me.

Nashville loved my dad.

And I loved Nashville.

John Rich came onstage and sang "Raising McCain," and then his hit "Save a Horse, Ride a Cowboy," and then a few other songs, all of which I danced to, with great joy and abandon and happiness, I'm told, but which I am sad to say I was too drunk to remember.

We were all crazy hungover the next day. But no hangover has ever been so sweet.

18

THERE ARE NO SECRETS

AFTER NASHVILLE, SWEET NASHVILLE, WE TRAVELED TO SEVEN STATES IN TWO WEEKS STRAIGHT, ON THE BUS, IN PLANES, AND SOMETIMES IN A big disgusting fifteen-passenger van—if my dad's campaign needed all the buses. The blog was going full tilt and so were we, doing campaign events every day, getting the hang of it, finding a groove. We went to Pennsylvania, New York, Massachusetts, Maine, and Ohio, Ohio, Ohio, Ohio.

The more we circled Ohio, the more we laughed, and danced, and hugged, and loved Ohio. How nice are those people?

Heather's faking-it strategy, that we look happy, even jubilant, became a self-fulfilling prophecy. Our bus tour of the heartland was a raging blast, and would eventually bring some of my happiest memories of the campaign.

We were like a family—Melissa, Frank, Meghan, Shannon, Heather, Josh, and Jay—and had our inside jokes, practical jokes, and silly jokes. We were always laughing, making the most of it. We gave our road trip a nickname, "The Shut It Down Tour," because we were going to have so much fun, and be so raucous and spirited, that we'd shut it down wherever we went. The *London Times* described us as the only happy people on the presidential campaign. When I look at pictures from those days, I am standing in a pumpkin patch in Maine with a huge smile on my face. I am cheerily reading *My Dad, John McCain* to a grade-school class.

Our posts were so upbeat and happy, in fact, we started to get e-mails and calls from stressed-out staffers back in headquarters telling us how jealous they were. We were having all the fun—and they were having none. The pitch of their voices was strained. They talked too fast and their attention span had dwindled to a few seconds before the conversation inevitably returned to one topic: Sarah Palin. She was turning out to be somebody who leaves a wake of confusion and chaos—to the point of dizziness—wherever she went.

Katie Couric's interview with her before the vice presidential debate had been disastrous. Unhappy with her performance, Palin seemed to blame the interview on the campaign. And she continued to blame other poor interviews and snafus on the campaign too. Under immense stress, she had lost her appetite and, like my mom and dad, was losing weight. Worrying about Sarah, my mom suggested that she come to the ranch in Sedona to decompress and do her debate prep there.

Her performance at the debate was terrific, but the sense of media frenzy and gossip around Sarah only grew. "The Time Bomb" was still ticking, and ticking, and valuable media coverage about substantial issues of the campaign gave over to intense fascination with Sarah— her personality, her looks, her sex appeal. It's hard to say it any other way except that Sarah became the story, not the campaign. The story was Sarah, and not the war, the economy, or health care, or what kind of president my dad would be. She attracted so much attention that it became counterproductive—distracting, distressing, and the message of the campaign became lost.

My dad never complained, not once, about Sarah or the attention she got. He seemed genuinely happy about both. It was left to the Groomsmen to work out any problems with getting the message out, and dealing with Sarah—and her own growing unhappiness. But they didn't seem to know how.

The campaign split into two camps—and were taking shots at each other. The main problems emerging, as far as I could tell, were that Sarah had no experience with a national presidential campaign but didn't seem to acknowledge it. She stuck to her gut, and the way things were done in Alaska, and second-guessed many of the decisions being made. But the Groomsmen didn't like being second-guessed. No big surprise there. They had been running this campaign for a long time by then, and most of them had been in national politics for decades. If Steve Schmidt had a different personality, he might have eased the tension and tried harder to get along. But Steve being Steve only made things worse.

WE WERE IN DENVER WHEN I CELEBRATED MY TWENTY-fourth birthday. My mom had flown in for some campaign events and then came to celebrate with me in my room at Brown's Hotel. Heather was taking pictures for the blog when Mom appeared in a powder blue bathrobe—wanting to wish me happy birthday. Heather quickly offered to put her camera away. She wanted to make sure Mom felt comfortable.

"Oh, I don't care," Mom said, "go ahead and take pictures. It's Meghan's birthday!"

Which is how pictures of my mother in a blue bathrobe made it onto the blog. She brought me a fantastic fake-fur Juicy Couture jacket for a present. Lindsey Graham dropped by to give me a hug. And room service arrived with a sheet cake and candles. But honestly, the best birthday present of all was hanging with Mom, relaxed and sweet and not caring how she looked.

We sat down on the bed together and caught up. Since my bus

tour had started, I hadn't been alone with her and my dad much, if at all. We'd gone to public events together, where I shared them with dozens of advisers and supporters. But it wasn't the same. My banishment from the main campaign had driven a wedge between us, but when I stepped back and looked at what was really happening, our separation wasn't about me. They were busy, caught up in the campaign, and working as hard as they could.

The stress was hard to imagine, and getting worse. Just the day before, the Republican National Committee had confirmed that it had spent $150,000 to dress the Palins for the campaign.

They needed clothes, no doubt. What they'd arrived with, in their bags from Alaska, just wasn't going to hold up in the harsh light of a national election. Look at the unbelievable focus that Michelle Obama's wardrobe had gotten, with every J.Crew sweater set and sleeveless dress discussed and swooned over.

I wasn't surprised by the price. That's what it costs to outfit seven or eight people in designer clothes. Other candidates had spent just as much, or more, but kept those kinds of expenses under wraps—sunk into promotion and advertising costs. What surprised me was that our campaign couldn't do the same.

Sarah had never been anything but pleasant to me. This almost made it harder to sort out all the complicated feelings I had about her. On a personal level, our contact had been limited. She and I did not have meals together, or travel much together. Our one-on-one exchanges were brief. I'd asked her to please tell Bristol to call me if she needed anything—anything at all—or just wanted to talk.

"I know how it feels," I said.

Nothing ever came of it. Things between our families hadn't really jelled either. It probably sounds naïve, but I had thought we would become one big happy family, warm and close, like the Partridge Family on tour. I was shocked when it wasn't like that—and might never be. I wondered if the tension of the campaign was driving everybody apart. And if Dad won, I supposed things would have to change. Wouldn't Bristol and I become friends?

I had asked Sarah if Bristol and her baby would be coming to live at the vice president's mansion in DC, and Sarah had said, "Yes! It would be such an amazing experience."

I wasn't sure what was normal—or supposed to happen between a president's family and a vice president's. But I know what I wanted: for everybody to get along.

My mom had a similar impulse. She reached out to the Palins and I don't think she always felt they had reached back. Words fell through the cracks. Offers to help—and bond—went unrecognized. My mom really hit it off with Todd, and liked her time with him, and both my parents were incredibly supportive of Bristol and Levi. My mom had even suggested that she and my dad would love to be godparents to their baby, if they were interested. But she never got an answer.

A part of me loved Sarah—and how comfortable she was creating waves. She brought so much life and juice and energy to the campaign. When she appeared at events with my dad, the crowds tripled and quadrupled. She seemed to enjoy doing her own thing—"going rogue"—and I have to confess that I enjoyed how she took on Steve Schmidt and didn't let him treat her like a dumb woman. He was used to snapping his fingers and making women jump. But she wouldn't jump.

On the other hand, she wasn't much of a team player, was she? The more I saw of her, the more perplexed and fascinated I was. And it was only the beginning of a very long roller coaster ride as I tried to make up my mind about her, and never could.

I'll confess, the swirl of chaos that October made me nostalgic about my birthday the year before in New Hampshire, when Heather had gotten up incredibly early and decorated the campaign van with Hawaiian leis, fake palm trees, streamers, and a pin-the-tail-on-the-donkey game. And we went to Ruby Tuesday for dinner, where I loved the salad bar. It was a simple birthday, and the beginning of an amazing year—spent entirely on the road campaigning. It felt like a really long time. And I'd learned so much. I felt one hundred years older.

"Remember last year?" I said to Mom.

She looked in my eyes and seemed to know that I was just barely keeping it together. The rest of our visit was upbeat, and Mom kept the conversation positive and constructive. The more stressful a situation is, the more focused she becomes on the things that really matter. This is probably the secret of her endurance, and how she's survived as a political spouse. The harder things are, the stronger she becomes.

"Just hold your head high," Mom said. "Keep a sense of dignity—no matter what happens."

Such simple advice, and so useful. If only I could remember to follow it, the way my mom always does.

19

THE ART OF TALKING POINTS

A RE WE GOING TO LOSE?
ARE WE?
IS IT SARAH PALIN'S FAULT?

I WAS DOING A TV INTERVIEW WITH A LOCAL DENVER affiliate, a day or two after my birthday. Melissa had coached me beforehand. The magic trick to doing television was remembering a list of things you wanted to say, or were supposed to say—aka *talking points*—and finding sneaky ways to weave them seamlessly into the interview. This sounds easy but it's not. I had been practicing and practicing on my book tour, but was only incrementally better.

Artistry is involved. There are definitely masters of talking points, people who can control the interview and have their say, no matter what topic is raised. The better you are, the more gracefully and seamlessly you are able to slip the talking points into your responses.

It's performance art and, like acting, it is about conveying something real and authentic while saying rehearsed lines and, in my case, regurgitating campaign speak. It was the last stop in fake—and the sort of thing I usually rail against. But I was determined to get better.

GOD LOVE MELISSA. I WOULD HAVE RUN FROM TV IN-terviews if it weren't for her. She encouraged me, kept my sanity alive. She hadn't asked to be assigned to me, I'm sure—handling press for a banished daughter-of must have been the lowest press job on the campaign. But Melissa never balked, complained, or treated me with anything less than respect and care. People had even started calling her "The Meghan Whisperer," because she had a spooky way of getting inside my head and convincing me to do things that nobody else could. Melissa is sensitive and, like me, maybe too sensitive for politics. She had a sixth sense about how I was doing and—even more amazing—where I was headed. She was unusually good at catching me when I wandered, or stumbled. But that day, I wandered so quickly, it was impossible to help.

The reporter with the Denver station was a really nice woman, and asked me an innocent, easy question—something anybody with half a brain could have answered without causing controversy. I don't think in a million years that she was trying to manipulate me or wanted me to make a fool of myself. But I did anyway.

She asked me about Sarah Palin. The reporter was only trying to discuss Sarah's immense popularity and all the excitement about her. It was an easy lowball.

"You must really like Sarah Palin," the reporter said, "and be so excited to have her as your dad's running mate."

But that list of talking points that Melissa and I had rehearsed was suddenly gone from my brain. I had lots of nice things to say about Sarah, but increasingly, I had doubts about her too. This made me not want to discuss her at all. So I said something dismissive, like, "Sarah Palin and I are very different women."

Not an obvious blooper, I realize. Not something that anybody ran to post on YouTube as a thigh-slapping gaffe to embarrass my dad's campaign. But if you study this remark under the giant magnifying glass of TV, as I had learned to do, it was obvious that I was distancing myself from my father's running mate when the general election was only a week away. I was calling into question, actually, whether I even liked her.

This wasn't a place that a daughter-of should ever go. I worried that one of the Groomsmen would call and complain, but luckily, they never seemed to notice.

Later, when I looked back on that day I realized it was when I first thought we could lose. And if we did, I wondered if it was Sarah Palin's fault.

★

COULD WE REALLY LOSE?

Could we?

I just refused to believe that.

Or could I?

★

IT BOTHERED ME HOW CRUEL THE BLOGOSPHERE WAS about my dad. He was painted as an old white guy, and so out of it that he didn't know how many houses we owned.

All the counts against him didn't seem like big negatives to me. People kept saying how old he was. Could he keep up? Did he have enough energy? What if something happened to him and Sarah Palin had to take over?

In our family, we never really thought Dad's age was a big deal, until the media kept pointing it out. To us, he was the man who was passionate about his work, the man who could hike farther than anybody, who kept the most grueling campaign schedule of all. Anybody who can keep a schedule like his was obviously not an "old" man.

Just eight years before, in 2000, he had been a darling of the media, a Washington renegade. But now the media seemed to urgently need him to be a different person—not daring or exciting, or even a war hero, but a tired "Washington insider" who, like all Republicans, was tainted by the unpopular Bush administration and everything that went along with that.

I didn't recognize Dad anymore when I watched the news—or read the political blogs. To me, my father is an iconic figure, outspoken and honest, an old-school American hero. His character had been strengthened by the unimaginable things he'd been through. To be honest, I wasn't able to read his memoir, *Faith of Our Fathers*, which includes descriptions of being a prisoner of war in Vietnam. The thought of my dad having to endure something like that . . . well, it was just too hard for me, too painful, to read about. Someday, I would. But I wasn't ready yet.

I didn't see how anyone couldn't believe in him as I did. Even with all the shortcomings of the campaign and all the missteps, at the end of the day, I believed that he was the more qualified man. He had the experience to run the country, and the strength to fight. He is realistic about the scary times that we live in. As a member of a much younger generation, I thought my father's experience would trump everything else in the end.

I thought that people would look at his résumé, at everything he had done in the Senate—and see him as the safer, better choice.

Running for president wasn't supposed to be like *American Idol*. But with each presidential election, each decade, appearance and coolness seemed to matter more. It wasn't just the candidates. The whole family had to be gorgeous, and media-genic. Was the most qualified candidate the most beautiful one, and the one who was so hip that he had Jay-Z on his iPod?

I was sure America wouldn't let the best man get away.

20

MY LOHAN MOMENT

THE MOMENTUM KEPT SWELLING AND SWELLING. THE PRESSURE NEVER SUBSIDED. THE WEEK BE-FORE ELECTION DAY WAS AN ALL-CONSUMING, nonstop, flat-out, scary, white-knuckle roller coaster ride of rallies, traveling, insomnia, candy bars, Diet Cokes, and stress. If there was a medical instrument that could gauge adrenaline levels, the entire campaign would have been hospitalized.

Mom urged me to take a few days off and catch up on my sleep after drifting off my talking points in Colorado and then dealing with the minor furor it caused. But, all due respect to Mom, "taking a break" from a campaign ten days before the general election is like trying to go to bed early the night before Christmas. You are so wound up, so excited, so strung out and addicted to sugar and the pace of the season, you lie awake in your bed and count every second until dawn.

I suffered through a long weekend of downtime, but it was pure agony to be away from the excitement. I joined up with my mom and dad and the main campaign on a swing through Colorado, then my bus-mates and I spun off to Nevada for two days of our own events, where glamorous Linda Ramone, the widow of singer Johnny Ramone, met up with us in Las Vegas. After a day of campaigning, Josh, Shannon, Frank, and I went on the Big Shot ride at the Stratosphere. I still have the picture of us in my apartment.

LIKE ALL BIG MEDIA EVENTS—LIKE THE OLYMPICS— there is a lot of attention leading up to election day. While the news attention had been pretty intense for the last two months, now, suddenly, the media was preoccupied with everything about the campaign and everywhere we went. It was like the way some people watch a football game only in the last quarter or the Indy 500 for just the last twenty laps.

Somebody—I'm not sure who—had the brilliant idea that we should milk this media focus as much as possible. On the day before the election, rather than having the campaign hit two states, like morning events in Ohio and an afternoon rally in Arizona, it was decided that Dad should go to seven cities in twenty-four hours.

When I first heard about this plan, I thought it was some kind of a joke.

Seven cities. It's hard to communicate what this means, in terms of logistics. My dad and mom. The campaign staff, the media traveling with us. Seven arrivals. Seven airports. Seven venues. Seven flights. I could go on and on, but you get the idea. This was supposed to be a brilliant way to make a final push of momentum.

But let's talk about the psychological condition of the staff by that point. For the last month, everybody had been getting by on three or four hours of sleep. Day after day, they were up, down, rallying, up, down, rallying. Just hearing the words *bag call* alone was a form of torture. Add to this, a diet of Coke, Snickers bars, and ramen Cup Noodles, and you can imagine how pleasant everybody was.

As for me, I was numb—almost disconnected from my body. My

mind was saying one thing and my body was up to something completely different. It was like jet lag. But since it was the last twenty-four
hours of my dad's campaign, I signed up for the seven-city tour: Tampa,
Blountville, Moon Township, Indianapolis, Roswell, Henderson, and
Prescott.

It sounded brutal.

It sounded excruciating.

But I didn't want to miss it for the world.

THE NIGHT BEFORE, WE HAD ARRIVED INCREDIBLY LATE
into Miami for a giant final rally at one in the morning. An entire
arena was filled up with people singing, dancing, and applauding for
my dad. There was so much energy and spirit and passion in the air
that, while waiting for my dad to appear onstage, people were doing
conga lines in the field and along the aisles.

It was three in the morning before we got back to our hotel that
night—or later—and even though I was zombie-tired, I was too jazzed
up to sleep. It was a common problem for everybody on the campaign.
In order to stay awake for late night rallies, you'd down caffeine. But
when it was over, you couldn't sleep.

I couldn't unwind, and when I did, I thought about the conga
lines and the cheering. The rally had been incredible, and I could tell
by the way Dad gave his speech that he was feeling energized and
upbeat. But the plans for the next forty-eight hours were daunting. If
my mind had remained focused on just this, I would have been okay.

But instead, I couldn't stop thinking about how the campaign was
almost over. And as much as I wanted it to be over, I couldn't imagine
it. The campaign was my whole life. Or, I mean, I could barely remember what my life had been like before. College was a vague
memory, like it had happened to somebody else.

I was caught up in something, and fired up, in a way I had never
been. I had fallen in love with politics, the day-to-day logistics of a

campaign as well as the philosophical battles and complicated issues that were hard to talk about. I even loved the inner-office dramas, bag calls, and excruciating hours as much as the roar of the crowds and roller coaster.

Maybe it was a form of Stockholm Syndrome, but I was scared to have it end. I knew how much I'd miss the whole thing. And while a part of me wanted it to be over, so I could wash myself completely of the experience, I was also beginning to see that the last year had been impossibly beautiful and moving and difficult and some of the scars I had might never heal.

And what if we won? We were going to win, I told myself, but that scared me too. Was I really ready? If I kept falling apart during a national election, how could I handle being a First Daughter?

And if we lost? You weren't supposed to think that way. You were supposed to stay positive, and energized, and confident. Deep down, I heard only whispers of doubt. It was easy to ignore them.

Mostly I was anxious, so anxious. "I am never going to be able to sleep!" I yelled out. "All I want is some sleep!"

I'm very anti-drug and never take them but over the summer, a friend of mine, who shall remain nameless, had given me some Xanax pills in an envelope with the words IN CASE OF EMERGENCY written in red marker. They were pills for anxiety, she said. While I appreciated the gesture, I insisted that I would never take anything like that.

But now I was fishing them out. It seemed as good a time as there would ever be. They worked instantly—but maybe that was all in my mind. I mean, literally within minutes of gulping down the pills with water, I was knocked out like a corpse, still in my clothes and makeup from the rally.

Bag call came three hours later, at six in the morning. Oh man. I was zonked. I would have been in full body pain if I'd actually been able to feel anything.

I struggled out of bed and groggily took a shower. Somehow I managed to put on a pair of tights and a stretchy jersey dress. It was the only thing left in my wardrobe that fit. I wasn't just heavier, I was bloated. My hands were so swollen that my rings had stopped fitting.

Josh came into the room to fix my hair. Sitting up in a chair, while he worked on it, I passed out cold—doubled over with my head down. He let me sleep while he stepped outside on the balcony to have a cigarette, but wound up locking himself out. No matter how hard he banged on the door, I never woke up. And eventually Heather and Shannon had to rescue him.

I don't remember getting my hair done, to be honest. Nor do I remember getting in the van to the airport. Getting on the airplane is also a big blur, but Shannon and Josh say they had to walk me down the aisle while holding on to my shoulders. When my shoes flew off my feet, they had to scramble to find them.

Once in my seat, located in the media section of the plane, I promptly passed out.

This is where I want to say a big THANK YOU to the media, after all the bashing that they've taken in this book, because nobody on that plane wrote about—or even seemed to care—that I was drugged unconscious after my first, and very pathetic, foray into the prescription drug world. (Later on, I heard that Cynthia McFadden had pulled aside a campaign staff member after seeing me and had said, "I understand pharmaceuticals are involved." So I want to give her a special shout-out for not putting it on *Nightline*.) How much the other reporters saw, or actually knew but kept to themselves, I don't know. But whatever leniency I was granted, I want to say that I appreciate every bit of it.

I also want to say a big THANK YOU to Melissa, who threw a blanket over my head when the plane landed at its first stop and members of the media shuffled passed me. Her fear was that somebody would take pictures.

Melissa is a genius, just in case I haven't given you that impression yet.

Under my blanket, I slept through the first three rallies of election day. But after that, my friends began to worry that I might be comatose.

Somebody called Dr. Harper, a physician who was traveling with the campaign and a longtime and very close family friend—a wonderful and very serious man whom I have known since I was a child. I was barely conscious, but just enough to make it one of the most humiliating experiences of my life. *"It's the last day of my dad's campaign and I can't move my legs. Am I going to be okay, Dr. Harper?"*

He determined that I would be fine, as long as I didn't take anything more. This was especially good news because it meant that my mother and father, who were traveling in the far front of the plane—and had enough things on their minds that day—didn't need to be informed of my condition. Actually, to this day I don't believe that my dad has been told about what my friends would later refer to as my "Lohan Moment." Until now. (Hi, Dad. I love you.)

By the time our plane got to Indianapolis, our fourth stop, I was coming alive again. I pulled myself together enough to attend the rally, which began at two o'clock. But when I came onstage with Dad, I was still woozy and dreamy-feeling, and remember looking out to the crowd and thinking, *Wow, so many nice older faces! And how happy they look!* This seemed like a wonderful sign—the fulfillment of brilliant campaign strategy. Older people vote in higher numbers, and tomorrow I imagined that all those great oldsters around the country would be getting up at the crack of dawn and flooding into voting booths to cast their ballot for Dad. There was no way we could lose.

I am an eternal optimist. Did I mention that? And I couldn't wait to see Mr. MIT proved wrong. Election day was just hours away and I was utterly sure we could win.

MY DAD'S SPEECHES ON THE LAST DAY HAD SO MUCH passion and love in them. He always speaks with his heart, and that day, it really came across. My favorite part of the speech was the final line—"We're Americans, and we fight! Never surrender! Never give up!" Music would play, either Journey's "Don't Stop Believin'" or "Life

Is a Highway" by Tom Cochrane. I still have a hard time listening to those songs even now.

There is a line from "Life Is a Highway" that I love: "Through all these cities and all these towns. It's in my blood and it's all around. I love you now and I loved you then." And Tom Cochrane screams, "Just tell them we're survivors!"

That was exactly how I felt. I loved my father as the candidate back in 2000 and I loved him that much more in 2008. I wanted to scream at the cynics and the people with their Hope and Change T-shirts. We were survivors! This fight wasn't over—and the road didn't end here.

WE FLEW AROUND THAT DAY IN THREE PRIVATELY CHAR-tered airplanes. The conditions were similar to the three buses that were used on the ground. There was a very nice, very large 737, where my mom and dad sat, as well as the Groomsmen and other important staff and media. A second 747, also very nice, was for the press and other staff.

And then, there was a third plane. It was a much smaller puddle-jumper—smellier, older, and skinny to the point of being tu-bular. This was no-man's-land, the Island of Misfit Toys in the air. The sound guys and boom operators were assigned this plane, and other out-of-the-loop techies. There were journalists from unknown publi-cations, or journalists who had been unfairly negative, taken potshots, had interrupted at press conferences, or were just unpopular and irri-tating to be around.

It shouldn't be a huge surprise where I wound up, except Mr. Burns had nothing to do with it.

I asked to be there.

That's right. I begged for that third plane. After being revived in the back of the first plane, I was going crazy listening to journalists and staffers sitting all around me and talking about poll numbers, what the Obama campaign was doing (only two rallies that day), and complaining endlessly about anything and everything. I wanted to get away from the know-it-all vibe.

Ahhh, the crummy third plane. It was small and cramped and the toilet smelled really bad and only worked half the time. When it was broken it made that annoying continual flushing sound. None of that mattered.

It was a paradise to me. It was quieter and my fellow travelers weren't drunk on power. They were laid-back and fun-loving and had the best "on the road" stories. One cameraman told me all about his former life as a Chippendale's dancer. This was stuff you don't get from *Wall Street Journal* reporters, believe me.

But with three more cities, and three more rallies to go, I was exhausted. At one point, while standing in line to get back on the plane, I asked Anna Marie Cox, a *Time* magazine blogger, if it was normal to do this many events on the last day. "No, Meghan, it's not!" she answered.

It reminded me of the fairy tale "The Red Shoes," where the girl puts on the magic red ballet slippers to dance, but then realizes she can't stop dancing—and eventually dances herself to death. It was a morbid vision, but suddenly it was all that I could think about. I was wearing campaign shoes that were making me walk, and walk, and walk. They were making me stand, and stand, and stand. Wave and wave and wave. It felt like it would never end.

21

ELECTION DAY

THIS IS WHAT I REMEMBER ABOUT ELECTION DAY:
I WOKE UP IN MY PARENTS' GUEST APARTMENT
IN PHOENIX WITH NO MEMORY OF HOW I GOT
there.

It was afternoon already. I had missed the entire morning of media craze. Shannon and Heather were hanging out, waiting for me to wake up, and John King's face was on CNN. He was doing his bizarre screen moves, when he touches his big magic screen and zeros in on certain counties and states and exit polls.

I took a shower and picked out a dress to wear. Trying to imagine what kind of night was ahead, I decided to wear something celebratory and fun—that way I'd be dressing for the occasion that I hoped for, not necessarily the one I'd get. It wasn't a hard decision. The one true constant of my clothing choices for the campaign was something glittery, something with sequins. Long ago I had decided it was always better to dress up than down. And there was no way on a night this big and important that I was going to wear a suit.

We could still win, couldn't we?

Couldn't we?

The dress was so beautiful—knee-length, gold and glittery with sequins everywhere and a gold bow across the waist. It was probably more acceptable for a night on the town in Vegas than election night but it was just what I needed. Josh helped me get my hair in a very curly, extravagant updo.

I decided to walk upstairs by myself to say hello to everyone in my parents' apartment. I wanted to see my dad and wish everybody good luck. I assumed that we had a very long night ahead of us. Like I've said, election days and nights were boring and kind of dreadful, since the call usually wasn't made until the middle of the night. And it wasn't impossible that it could go on for days, like the presidential election of 2000, when the vote in Florida had to be recounted. I had a hunch that this time, it was going to be a close election too.

I entered the apartment in a very cheery mood, full of energy, and looking forward to seeing everyone. Inside, besides my family—my parents, brothers, and sister, my grandmother—the usual suspects were standing around: Steve Schmidt, Rick Davis, Charlie Black, Brooke Buchanan, and Blond Amazon, along with an assortment of my parents' assistants, close staffers, the advance team, and of course, the Secret Service.

Something was wrong, though. Everyone was just standing around, kind of dead and super-still. Nobody was moving. It was like they'd been frozen in place. Political people were never quiet or motionless like this, when gathered together. They were always talking on their phones, checking their BlackBerrys, moving around the room, schmoozing. Maybe that's why they were called "movers and shakers," because people in politics never just *stood around*.

We must be losing.

What I didn't know was that we'd already lost.

Dan Yeary, the pastor of our church, North Phoenix Baptist, must have noticed the look on my face. He came up to me and grabbed my hand and said, "Everything happens for a reason, Meghan. God always has a plan."

I walked into the kitchen, looking for Dad. I was told to go out on the balcony in the other room. He needed to talk to me. When I found him, my brothers, Jack and Jimmy, and my sister, Bridget, were already there.

Dad pulled us into a semicircle, like a huddle before a football game. I was hoping that this was some kind of sign that he knew a secret—a poll or voting area that hadn't been reported.

No, that wasn't it.

"Look, guys," he said. "It seems we're not gonna win this thing." That was it. I don't remember a lot else, except I thought I'd lose it immediately but I didn't. I hugged my father, told him how proud I was of him, and just walked straight out the door like a robot. I went downstairs to the other apartment, where Shannon and Heather and Josh were waiting, and I told them what happened.

"What?"

"It's only five o'clock!"

Polls hadn't closed; people were still voting all over the country, pulling the lever for my dad. But the campaign's internal polling was already sure that he had lost.

I hated the way it was ending. *Election nights are supposed to go on and on.* You were supposed to be up until the middle of the night, dead on your feet and still waiting to hear the news.

Five in the afternoon wasn't the way it happened.

The sun wasn't even down.

My dad hadn't even eaten dinner.

What about Florida? And Ohio? *What the hell happened in Ohio?* I knew that state so well; it felt like I'd been to every single county, every small town and city, traveled on every highway, byway, service road, visited every possible Cracker Barrel, Olive Garden, and Applebee's, and met with God only knows how many people.

What about Ohio?

I hadn't seen this coming—at all. Even in my darkest moments, I figured we had a great chance to win because my dad was so obviously the better choice, the more experienced and dependable leader. Everywhere we went people had been so excited about the election, and excited about my dad. Those conga lines in Miami, the screaming crowds in Indianapolis. Even in the desperate pitch of the stupid seven-city tour of nonstop rallies, deep down I believed that we couldn't lose.

The feeling of heartbreak was so crushing, so painful, and I blamed myself for not being better prepared for it. If only I were more thick-skinned. Maybe that way I'd be inoculated from ever feeling this wounded again.

What about friggin' Ohio?

The only thing that I remember doing between five o'clock, when the news of our defeat began to drill its way into me, and the time that I was due back upstairs to regroup with my family for an appearance at the Arizona Biltmore, was holding Melissa's hand. I grabbed Melissa's hand and never let it go.

ON THE WAY BACK TO MY PARENTS' APARTMENT, UP-stairs, I broke down in the hallway where the Secret Service were standing, and it made it so much worse that they'd seen me like that.

Upstairs, my dad called out for everybody—family and campaign staff—to gather in one room and he thanked them for the great work they had done for him, and for "just being there." With a calm voice and no sign of being devastated, he even remembered to thank the Secret Service, which really got me. They were nowhere near the top of my thank-you list, but of course, my dad included them too.

Outside, there was a lineup of big SUVs waiting at the curb. My parents got in the first one, along with Lindsey Graham and me. Just looking at Lindsey made me fall apart, and I started crying on his jacket sleeve.

Somebody mentioned being upset about the Hispanic vote going to Obama. During the early parts of the campaign, my father took hits for his stance on immigration, and Lindsey was right there with him. Some people even started writing "José McCain and Lindsey Gomez" on protest signs. This seemed to be the final sting for Lindsey and Dad. Nobody had seen that one coming.

As we turned into the Arizona Biltmore, a crowd of Obama supporters were standing on a corner with big Obama signs and jeering at our motorcade. They were so pumped up, feeling so good, but somehow still so angry. It was unimaginable to me how anyone would wait for us on the street so they could rub in their victory like that—and glare at the losers.

When I started to lose it again, my parents said, "Enough crying." Whatever happened, they told me not to cry in public—onstage or anywhere else. I had to be strong for my mom and dad and my younger siblings. I had to be dignified and not hand the media an opportunity to photograph me with tears streaming down my face. I thought of those jerks on the corner, jeering at us with their Obama signs, and I didn't want them to find a way to have more glory from our loss.

I asked God for help.

He heard me. Nobody saw me cry for the rest of the night.

Crowds were waiting for us at the hotel, and began clapping as we were ushered on foot to a private bungalow that the campaign was using for the night. The grounds of the Arizona Biltmore are beyond gorgeous—sprawling, manicured, three dozen acres of tamed Arizona desert. People were lined up along the pathways clapping. The hotel staff was gathered, and clapping. My dad led the way, and I could only see the back of his head, glimpses of him in the excitement.

Inside the bungalow, I saw Sarah Palin standing in the kitchen. She looked stunning in a deep blue dress with her hair pulled half up and half down, her signature semi-beehive style. I stopped to play with little Piper for a while. She was happy and jumping around, like most seven-year-olds, and didn't seem to know that we'd lost. I sure didn't want to be the one to tell her.

While I talked with Sarah, she was holding some papers in her hand, a speech, I assumed.

"Are you going to speak?" I asked her.

"I want to," she said, "but others don't agree."

"You look beautiful," I said.

When it came time for my father's concession speech, we had a long walk ahead of us—five minutes that seemed like an hour—to a place on the Biltmore grounds where a stage had been erected. I grabbed my little sister Bridget's hand. I remember gripping tightly as we walked together. There was more clapping, and more people lined up along pathways.

The warm welcome felt nice, but only momentarily. Looking ahead at my dad, I couldn't help but think about how this country that he loved so much, more than anything else in life, and had given so much to—this unbelievably intoxicatingly amazing country—did not want him.

It did not want my old father. It did not want my mother, whom it had never really known. It didn't want my brothers in the military or my beautiful soul of a sister. And it didn't want me—an over-bleached glitter girl in a too-happy gold dress on such a sad night. The rejection didn't feel intellectual or philosophical. It didn't seem like a bunch of ideas or a political party had been rejected. It felt really personal. It felt like us. We had been rejected. And the pain of this was a complete assault on my emotions and senses.

My dad wasn't enough and we weren't enough—not interesting or evocative or beautiful enough. And we weren't new.

I cracked a few jokes to push this out of my head. I made jokes about anything and everything. They were like old friends, these jokes. And they would get me through—I knew they would. And they would make Bridget feel better too.

"At least the Secret Service won't have to put up with me anymore."

"At least I will never have to eat a Snickers bar for breakfast again."

I could hear Bridget giggling, softly.

"I've gained so much weight that my Spanx are breaking at the seams."

Out of nowhere, Steve Duprey, the owner of the Concord Marriott, appeared and grabbed my hand. How did he get here? I hugged him. "Kid," he said, "we had some great times, didn't we?" Nobody has ever made me feel as good, or pulled me out of such a dark place. And best of all, unlike everybody else in my father's orbit that evening, Steve Duprey wasn't crying.

THE SKY WAS DARK AND CLEAR. AS WE WALKED ONTO the stage at the Biltmore, I looked up at the stars shining and they made me feel strong. Before us, the golf course of the hotel was a sea of people, mostly silent.

My dad started to speak. I looked at him standing next to Sarah Palin in her dark blue dress and thought, *I have to remember this*. I wanted to hold on to every single moment. The sky. The stars. The stage that was full of people I loved. *Don't forget. Don't forget.*

Dad was starting to look sad, but he would keep it together, he always did. When things were hard, he always said, "I've been through worse," and I knew that he was talking about being a prisoner of war. Back in the apartment he had said how lucky he felt to be part of a small group of people who had become a nominee for president. He always held on to his perspective. He held on to things that were good.

My father's speech was perfect, so beautiful, the most glorious concession speech, but listening to it was one of the hardest things I will ever have to do. Down below the stage, Heather was taking pictures of us—the way she always did—but her face was streaked with tears. I remember thinking how awful, how awful, *this is all so awful*, but at the same time thinking how beautiful too.

Caring about your country was beautiful. Finding hope in a leader was beautiful. Even losing was beautiful.

Then I looked out, beyond where Heather was, at the people gathered on the golf course to hear my dad. So many of them were crying; it was a sea of crying faces. I was so moved by this, so crushed, so happy. Look at how much people loved my dad, and loved politics, and loved this country. This counted for something. This counted for everything. There was so much love all around, and spirit, and faith. And I saw that I was lucky—so lucky—to be John McCain's daughter and to have been a part of this, the pain and the beauty. And above everything else, I saw that God had a plan and my father being president of the United States was not a part of it.

I don't really remember walking off the stage. Emotion can be like a drug and wipe everything out of your head. But I do remember being backstage and seeing Sarah Palin's mother crying hysterically—wailing, and making loud sobbing sounds and hugging little Piper. It was hard to witness. All the other Palins had their game faces on. They knew what their job was. But Sarah's mother couldn't do it.

Then, for some weird reason, Sarah stepped back onstage by herself. She was waving to the crowd, saying hi to the cameras, almost as though she were in Alaska—not Arizona. What was she doing? I was shocked. It was as if she wanted to make the night about her, and not my dad. She was trying to have the last word, and the last wave.

What else did she want or need? What was driving her to do this? Possibly it was unconscious, this dramatic bit of upstaging, and she couldn't see how it could look to us or anybody else. She was supposed to leave the stage, but she couldn't go along with the plans, even then—even on the last night—and just follow my dad and the rest of us back to the hotel bungalow. She didn't have a go-along side to her. And I saw something that I hadn't really wanted to see before: Losing wasn't an end for her. It was a beginning.

As for me, I was perfectly ready to say good-bye. Good-bye to the campaign. Good-bye to politics. Soon it would all be behind me. I told myself: My dad will never run for president again. I will never have to go through this again.

My father and family had given so much to the Republican Party over the years, but I didn't want to give anything more. The party couldn't see or admit how damaged it was. And I didn't want to stick around and watch it—losing its way, forgetting its heart, missing its chances, and completely missing the point. That night I was standing at its funeral and saying good-bye.

22

AND THEN THERE WAS ROCK BAND

I WOKE UP ALONE AND THE APARTMENT WAS QUIET, AN ECHOING SILENCE. SO THIS IS WHAT DEFEAT IS LIKE, I THOUGHT. NOTHING AND NOBODY AND NO sound.

We hadn't made plans for losing. In the mind-set of our family, if anybody had ever said, "This is what we'll do after we lose," it could have jinxed everything.

Plans for winning? Oh, we had lots of those. My father had spent the last two years talking about nothing else—all the things he was going to do when he won, the things to fix, the war, the economy, health care. But now the talking had stopped. The rallies were finished. And I woke up in my parents' guest apartment in Phoenix alone in bed and wearing my gold glitter dress and a smeared game face of election night makeup. I looked like I had been in a car accident.

My pain was dull but throbbing somewhere, way down inside me, like somebody had given me a shot of Novocain directly into my heart.

Where were my friends? They had gone, scattered off. Last I'd seen them, after the concession speech, they had come with me to the hotel bungalow for an after-party, where the campaign staff had gathered, the aides, the Bus Nazi, the Groomsmen. I was just trying to get through it, and looked for people whom I needed to thank and say good-bye to, like my tireless web designer, Rob Kubasko. But I lost heart very soon. I didn't even have the energy to drink much. I was too sad and in shock. I felt unreal, like a person I was watching in a movie.

Shannon, Heather, and Josh had already left by then. I assumed they had wandered back to the ballroom of the Biltmore, where a far larger mass of people—thousands of volunteers, staff, donors, coordinators, speakers, organizers—were doing a grieving/celebrating thing that just seemed way too painful for me. I was supposed to stop by. I said that I'd stop by. Instead, I had gone back to my parents' apartment building and fell asleep as soon as my head hit the pillow.

After a shower, I went downstairs in sweatpants and a sweatshirt and tried to find a car. I didn't care whose car or what car. My parents and a bunch of campaign staff had driven up to our cabin in Sedona—either very late on election night or early in the morning. The doorman brought around a Toyota Prius, the only family car left, and I drove it straight to the Biltmore to find my friends. I was in a crazy mood.

I didn't want to be alone, but I didn't want to see anybody either, except Shannon, Heather, and Josh. I needed them the way I've never needed friends before. But the press corps was staying at the hotel and, more than anything, I didn't want to be cornered and have to try to talk graciously about what it felt like to lose.

No more fake stuff.

I was done with that.

But while I was looking for my friends, I ran into Kelly O'Donnell, a TV reporter from NBC, and thankfully one of the normal people. Kelly was very sweet and sensitive, I remember that. But I couldn't wait to get away.

Shannon and Heather and Josh were in various states of fatigue and inebriation when I found them. They were starving, too. So I brought them back to the apartment and fed them lunch. They started talking about election night and the parties I had missed—the drinking, chain-smoking, the madness and crazy stuff.

I started feeling a little frantic, just thinking about all the people that I hadn't said good-bye to. All the people I might never see again. People who had meant so much to me. All gone, disbanded, people whom I had loved, and hated, and loved hating. You know what I mean. They had been my family and my whole world for seventeen months.

I hadn't done anything right.

I hadn't thanked enough people, or hugged enough people. The ending had slammed me. I had just survived it—like some kind of explosion—and not thought about anybody else but myself. I wondered when that would stop. When I grew up?

While we were eating, we turned on the TV—an addiction at this point. For the last four months it was always on, in every room, wherever we were. We expected to see Obama on the screen. But Sarah Palin was giving interviews in the lobby of the Biltmore. *What?* Why the hell was she giving interviews? Was the failed vice presidential running mate supposed to do that? My dad certainly wasn't giving interviews.

We were shouting at the screen. I think somebody threw a pillow. Sarah was trying to continue her political career, or save it, we figured, and separate herself from my dad and his loss. She was trying to be her own person now, free from us, free of the campaign and my dad. I don't know if that's what she was doing, or thinking, but we decided it was.

Our defeat was just hours old, and still too painful, to us anyway—*wasn't she even heartbroken?* But it was the very beginning of what would be months of postmortem, the beginning of Sarah and many individuals in the campaign not letting things die or the wounds heal. The fallout from the campaign went on and on and everybody except my dad would want to have their say. Including me.

Election night was like a fire, and when the ashes were left, there would be things that would rise out of them. Nothing is ever really over, it just evolves into something else.

I was supposed to drive up to meet my parents at the cabin in Sedona later that day. But I stalled—hating to say good-bye to my friends, hating to separate after all our months together. I couldn't stand to think about it. But they had their own lives and careers to get back to. I knew that. But I asked anyway. Would they stay a little longer, get me through the next few days? They weren't my employees anymore—staffers who were helping me with the blog or my hair. I was closer to them than I'd been to anybody.

They didn't just say yes. They said they wanted to stay with me and weren't ready to leave yet. I'm not sure they were telling the truth. But the gesture itself says everything. Shannon, Heather, and Josh stayed around to bring me back to life.

MY PARENTS HAVE A CABIN BETWEEN SEDONA AND COT-tonwood, about a two-hour drive from Phoenix. While I drove, Shannon, Heather, and Josh rehashed election night, everything I had missed.

The Biltmore ballroom had been a big wake and split up into many smaller wakes, which went on all night. The Originals, people who had spent two years of their lives completely devoted to the campaign, found each other like magnets and didn't let go. There was drinking and everything else, almost everything, including skinny-dipping in the Biltmore pool. I was hanging on every word my friends were saying, delighting in the gloriously bad behavior, until I saw blue and red lights swirling and flashing in the rearview mirror.

I was being pulled over.

The officer said I was going eighty-five mph. He asked why I was speeding.

"I'm sorry, Officer," I said, handing over my driver's license. "My dad just lost the election to Barack Obama."

This is possibly the best excuse I've ever had for speeding. He gave me a warning.

Pulling back onto the highway, our conversation started up again, including a long analysis of crazy-sex—and what it is about. I remembered meeting a guy once who had done a "semester at sea" in college, traveling around the world on a cruise ship and taking courses. He told me a story about how the ship had encountered a terrible storm, so bad that they all thought they were going to drown. People were praying and freaking out, and scrambling for life jackets. He said the only thing that he could think about was having sex one more time before he died. He went around to random girls and asked if they were interested. He didn't want to die doing anything else.

Election nights are kind of like that. The emotions are so strong and searing—the exhilaration or disappointment is overwhelming—and, no matter what, a part of your life is ending. Crazy-sex was a way to get through it, work it out, even honor and celebrate it. As much as my mom will be horrified to hear this, I understood what crazy-sex was about.

I wish that something so dramatic had happened to me, that my campaign celibacy vow had ended that very night—like the minute the campaign was over, I got drunk and tore off my clothes, skinny-dipped in the Biltmore pool, and then drifted off with a campaign staffer whom I had crazy chemistry with, and been attracted to the whole time, and then, we wound up together for the night. That would be the movie version. But there'd been no campaign staffer for me, not even one I'd had my eyes on. In reality, I went back home to the guest apartment and passed out in my gold dress.

The vow could end now, in any case. I was free to have sex again. When my sanity returned, life normalized, and I found somebody worth the trouble and risks, would it come back to me, after all these months?

Was it like riding a bike?

It was pitch dark when we arrived in Sedona. Our cabin is in the middle of the mountains, deep in a canyon, essentially in the wilderness. We crawled out of the car like bugs that have been hiding under a rock.

We were like boat people—scruffy, tired, needing showers and sleep. The main cabin was empty, as far as we could tell, or my parents were asleep. But I needed to find them so they could tell us where to stay.

Looking for them, I wandered into one cabin and pushed open a bedroom door and saw Charlie and Judy Black under the covers, curled up in bed.

"Oops! Sorry!'

I love Charlie and Judy, and there was something so funny, and so classic, about standing in a bedroom in my ragtag state and coming upon those two in their pajamas.

I laughed and couldn't stop. It meant so much to me.

My first post-election laugh.

THE NEXT MORNING MY DAD WAS SITTING BY THE POND, alone, making phone calls. The trees behind him were so beautiful, golden and red, autumn colors. The air was dry, chilly but sunny. He had a sheet of paper in front of him, a long list of names and phone numbers on it.

Just seeing him, like that, made me cry. There was something about how all alone he was too. The night before, he had been surrounded by what felt like millions of people and now he was all alone sitting by our pond with his sunglasses and dorky Dad sweatshirt on making phone calls and being stoic.

The aftermath. This was going to be the worst part, wasn't it?

I walked over to him slowly, told him I loved him, and gave him a hug.

Then I found my mom, and asked her what my father was doing, and she said that he was calling supporters and big donors to thank them. She looked really tired but hanging in there for all of us. She was wearing jeans and a sweater and I remember thinking it had been a long time since I'd seen her in cabin clothes, casual stuff, the kind of thing she liked to wear at home.

"Where is everybody?" I asked. Charlie and Judy, Steve Schmidt, Rick Davis, and everybody else had gone back to their families that morning. Only Brooke Buchanan, my dad's tireless press secretary, was left, along with my parents, my sister, Bridget, and my friends. My brother Jack had gone back to the Naval Academy that morning. My brother Jimmy was heading back to Camp Pendleton, where he was stationed.

That afternoon, my dad started grilling. It was his therapy. He grills steak, chicken, hot dogs, hamburgers, and basically any other kind of meat, poultry, and fish imaginable. He is a grill master, and loves feeding people. He loves it when we really load up our plates and keep coming back for more.

Suddenly food became the focus of our existence. We feasted as though we hadn't eaten in two years. Meat, big meals, everything he could grill, several times a day, and even though I started to feel really full, I kept eating. We only stopped to sleep.

Eating and sleeping.

Sleeping and eating.

We returned to the essentials. We let our bodies be exhausted. If you are doing nothing all day, you make more time for food.

Getting dressed seemed like a big effort, so we stayed in our pajamas all morning, and our sleepwear evolved to a form of in-between wear, comfort clothes like sweats and T-shirts, my ubiquitous UGG boots. We all looked raggedy and who-cares. After Brooke left for Colorado—to see her parents, her dog, Maddie, and go skiing—it was down to me and Bridget and my friends with Mom and Dad.

Sitting around the lunch table, we came up with a game called "What Cindy Did Next" where we dreamed up things for Mom to do now that the election was over. We decided that she should try out for *Dancing with the Stars,* and she smiled, her first smile since the election. We kept the idea alive for days until we'd almost convinced her.

After lunch, we slept.

We woke up, and ate again.

Dad's dry ribs. This would be my last meal if I had to pick a last meal. And I ate his dry ribs like it was. He grills them with lemon, garlic, and other "secret ingredients." It takes hours and hours and always reminds me of my childhood. Dad grilled an onion for me too, he always does, because I love, love, love onions so much. This is his special thing, just for me: an onion wrapped in tin foil with a lemon on it.

And then, we discovered Rock Band.

WE WERE AVOIDING THE TV NEWS FOR THE OBVIOUS reasons. And after so many months of being obsessed with the news cycle, we wanted to see if we could live in a world without one. It was really strange at first. Somebody voted that we watch movies, but I nixed that idea, fearing they might be too emotional.

The big TV screen in the living room was looming over us, so we decided to try playing Rock Band. All the equipment was just sitting there, left by Bridget or my brothers. I had never played it, or anything like it, my entire life.

For those of you who don't know, Rock Band is a video game where the players use drums, a guitar, and a microphone to play along, or sing along, to rock music. It's a competition, and a tiny bit like karaoke, except you are judged by how well you can hit the notes on time, and sing the words. Actual talent is beside the point.

Once we got into it, there was no stopping us. Hour after hour, day after day, we played Rock Band in the living room—from the moment we woke up, after going into town for Starbucks coffee. My dad would be grilling outside on the deck, and inside, in our pajamas, we played Rock Band.

We took turns trying all the instruments—the guitar, and singing parts, and the drums. Then a pattern developed, where Heather played the drums because she was a drumming savant—the minute she first tried them. Shannon always got to sing the Courtney Love songs, and Josh played so much guitar that his fingers bled one day. He taped them up in Band-Aids and played on.

My best songs reminded me of the campaign, Garbage's "I'm Only Happy When It Rains" and Oasis's "Don't Look Back in Anger." I pretended I was Shirley Manson. I am really not a singer, at all, but when you don't care and just sing your heart out, it has a way of feeling like something real and compelling and transformative is happening in the room.

We took short breaks sometimes—just sat in the sun on the deck. Sometimes, if my dad wasn't on the deck, we'd talk about the election. When he was around, we didn't. Nobody did. You couldn't raise the subject. It was too painful.

Eventually we became so into Rock Band, it was the only thing we were able to think about. We lived to play. Our conversations started being only about Rock Band. We bickered over the singing and who wasn't hitting the notes. Sometimes my mom or dad would come into the living room and want to talk, and interrupt, but we just continued to play. We were Rock Band obsessives. One time, our neighbors in Sedona, the Harpers, came over and watched a bit, and made a few jokes with my parents about how into the game we were. But we were really serious about Rock Band by then, and didn't laugh along. To us, it wasn't a joke.

That was it. That's how we passed the time, in the dry air and sunshine of Sedona, in the shadow of the red cliffs. Instead of appointing a transition team and cabinet secretaries and inaugural chairperson, and giving thousands of volunteers and Republican staffers jobs in a new administration, and taking over the reins of power from George Bush, my dad grilled me onions and made his dry ribs. My mom laughed at the thought of being on *Dancing with the Stars*. I sang my heart out and played Rock Band with the best friends I ever had.

MOMENTS OF REALITY SEEPED INTO THE BUBBLE OF MY little world, though. Once, we went into town so Josh could cash his campaign check before going back to LA, and when the bank teller saw the check, issued by the McCain Campaign, she said we'd all done a brave job and she had voted for Dad, and Josh got emotional.

Another time, we went into town to get our nails done. The nail salon was really dinky, so we took turns, went in shifts, because there were too many of us to get done at once. Bridget was finished, and about to leave, when a woman in the salon asked her if she was "John McCain's adopted daughter."

Now, if you have ever met Bridget, who is sweet and incredibly modest, you would know instantly that she isn't into having a famous father.

"Yes, I am," Bridget said.

"He lost the election because of Sarah Palin," the woman snapped.

Bridget came to find me outside, where we were drinking our coffee, and she told me the story. Seeing Bridget was upset, Heather, who never loses her cool, became enraged. We call Heather "Little Buddha" and things like that, because she is a laid-back Californian and Zen personified. But she went striding into the nail salon and found the woman and asked, in a loud voice, if she was the one who'd just been talking to Bridget.

"Who are you?" the woman asked defensively.

"I'm Heather."

I'm Heather. As if that made a difference to anybody. And then Heather started yelling. "This family is going through a really hard time—can't you imagine that? And this is the first time they are venturing out into the world and you start laying into a seventeen-year-old girl about why her dad lost the election? That is so uncool, so insensitive. *What's wrong with you?*"

Bridget and I were hugging each other in the car. After a few minutes we started to drive away and Shannon and Heather rolled down the windows and turned up the radio. I don't remember what the song was exactly, something cheesy like Britney Spears's "Toxic."

The car picked up speed and the dry high desert air rushed in and blew on our faces. We were singing at the tops of our lungs. Singing at the blue sky. Singing at the mountain and the lush canyon.

Arizona is my home. I was back home again. The campaign could crush me and take over my life or I could find a way to be better for it. I inhaled the fresh dry high desert air. My wounds were open, and still sore, and I was feeling alive again.

23

NOW WHAT?

I T WAS THE MOST HISTORIC ELECTION IN RECENT
MEMORY, WITH MORE PEOPLE TURNING OUT TO VOTE
THAN EVER BEFORE. THE YOUNG VOTED—WITH EX-
citement, enthusiasm, and incredible passion. They organized. They
contributed. And they proved that they care about their future, about
politics, about this beautiful country and its place in the world. They
care about ideas and understand they are worth fighting for.

The problem was that the young—or two-thirds of them—voted
for the other guy and not my dad.

My dad got forty-eight million votes. That's not an embarrassment, but it wasn't enough to win. Did he lose because of Sarah Palin?
Did Obama win because of Joe Biden? No.

Obama was unbeatable, in my opinion. I believe that my father's
running mate—while she changed so many things about the race—
had no bearing on the outcome of the election. Obama was just too
appealing, a new messiah—a young, smart, good-looking politician
who represented everything that George W. Bush didn't.

★

THE ELECTION LEFT ME SHATTERED FOR A WHILE. I spent two months in my pajamas, pretty much, at home in Phoenix, a luxury that wasn't afforded my dad, who was back in his office in Washington almost immediately, catching up on his Senate obligations.

When I wasn't fogged out and numb, I wallowed in waves of dread and panic, and an unattractive fury, like something terribly unfair had happened in the world. It wouldn't have been a good thing to mention president-elect Barack Obama to me during that time.

I didn't know how my dad went on, plowing ahead without complaint. That's how he is. His interest in rehashing was zero. The rest of my family was moving on too, or trying. My mom plunged into charity work. My sister, Bridget, had school to focus on, as did my brother Jack, who was in his last year at the Naval Academy. Jimmy had been deployed, and was overseas on a ship. I was jealous of their commitment to things, and that they had duties and plans.

Not me. The only duty I had was the blog. But I was avoiding that. I kept telling myself that I would do a final post about election night, but I couldn't bring myself to. I couldn't put those sad pictures on the Internet, or even write about it. My feelings were still too raw and my heart just wasn't in it. As much as I wanted to pull the plug on McCainBlogette, I couldn't come up with a good game plan about how to do it. So instead, I just let it die off, a slow death.

Graduating from college leaves a lot of people at a crossroads. I had heard stories about friends who fell apart, felt lost or full of dread during their first year out. There was a hole—and too many choices—after years of working hard in a formal setting of a classroom, with the predictable schedule of lectures, tests, finals, the next semester always coming up.

Now the question facing me was the very thing that I had escaped by joining the campaign. What was I going to do with my life? What did I want? I never put it into words like that. It was mostly a feeling of emptiness. The hurricane was over, I had survived, and now what was I supposed to do?

A bunch of nothing is what I did. I slept in. I watched a ton of TV. I went out with friends and drank red wine. I walked our dogs. I rediscovered yoga and dating and getting to wear consistently clean clothes. Looking back, I'm sure I was depressed and exhausted, and my body was trying to readjust to normal life. Except, nothing seemed too normal anymore.

AT CHRISTMAS, I WENT ON VACATION WITH MY FAMILY. It was the first time we were all together since election night. Only a few months before, it had been hard to be physically near my dad, or be alone with him, because of the pressure of the campaign, his grueling schedule, and the omnipresent Secret Service agents. But suddenly it was like old times, just the six of us traveling in a pack again.

It is weird to go on a trip with my father. People don't know how to treat an ex-presidential candidate. There is an awkward reaction to seeing him in person, and not surrounded by a bunch of handlers or Secret Service agents. The fact that he is surrounded only by my mom and me, my brothers and sister, is jarring for people. Maybe they are so used to seeing him on TV that they think he must go on vacation with the hosts of *Meet the Press* and *This Week*.

People always say they voted for my dad too. Wherever we go, no matter what, they'll say that. He's a famous politician, so they want to get up close and talk to him, but once they do, they can't think of anything else to say except that they voted for him, even if they didn't.

At Christmas, at LAX, where we were waiting for a flight, there was more commotion around him than usual. The election had only been seven weeks before and was still fresh in people's minds. Crowds formed around him, and people expressed emotion, and sometimes it felt very raw.

Even now, when people come up to me and say that they wish my father were president because "everything would be so different," it is hard to know what to say. They like to tell me why he lost—all of their theories—and blame it on Sarah Palin or George Bush. Meeting me, I guess, brings up strong feelings about politics and the campaign, about my dad, about Obama and his administration. They project their emotions and feelings on me, and I understand that. But it is difficult for me, too, and was especially so after the election.

All I wanted to do was forget about it. Like my dad always does, I wanted to do my best to move on.

But to what?

SINCE THE ELECTION, I HAVE FOUND MYSELF RELATING to my dad in so many new ways—and admiring what he has brought to politics and the party over the years. He has made a career of thinking for himself, and not accepting the status quo or groupthink. That's what got him the reputation for being a maverick.

But when I thought back on the campaign, and my own behavior, I cringed. There were things that I wished I'd done differently, and lots of things I wished I had never said. I'm not sure I handled the pressure and intense emotion as well as I could have. If only I had been more grown-up, or even just five years older.

Looking back, I believe a lot of my frustration was due to the constrained bubble world of a national campaign. I had been raised to speak my mind freely and be independent. If there was one thing that my dad wanted for me—and all his kids—it was to be strong, think for ourselves, and support ourselves. We were never supposed to rely on government or family money or a trust fund to take care of us. We were supposed to work, make a life for ourselves, and find a way to make things better around us.

But a national presidential campaign has to put forward one candidate—one agenda, one message, one set of views. The family of the candidate isn't supposed to disagree or offer alternatives. The spouses of the candidates have to remain pretty silent—and just go along with the script. My mom is miraculously good at this. But even an old hand at politics, like former president Bill Clinton when campaigning for his wife in 2008, gets in trouble if he says too much.

I understood the reasoning. In the white noise rising from the campaign and all the candidates participating, it is important to hear each candidate loudly and clearly. My father was running for president, not me or my mom. And it was important for voters to really know him, and his views. If there was a chorus of dissenting opinions or different voices emerging from the campaign, his voice would get drowned out.

And then there was the Republican Party to consider. It was one thing to toe the line for my dad, who loved and appreciated and respected me—in spite of our differences. I could do that. But it was another to toe the line for a party that I felt increasingly alienated from.

More than anything, the campaign experience had opened my eyes to the inner workings and culture of the Republican Party. It had its own platform and agenda and base. And increasingly, this base was becoming narrower and narrower. It was no longer the party of the individual.

It was no longer the party of fiscal conservatives. George Bush had grown the federal budget in an unprecedented way. Under his leadership, it had moved farther and farther Right too, and was now a huddling mass of groupthinkers. The base, although critical of Bush, was spending all its time in a corner—a Far Right corner—and as far as I could tell, if it wanted to keep losing elections, it should stay there. It was becoming unappealing to moderates and people of my generation, who were now passionately politicized and voting in record numbers. And it was completely unappealing to the cross-over electorate who had voted for Ronald Reagan in 1981.

What had happened to the party of *You Live Your Life and I'll Live*

Mine? What happened to the party that loved the notion of self-reliance and, my personal favorite, individualism? I couldn't help but yearn for the conservative philosophies of those two great men Barry Goldwater and Ronald Reagan, who believed it was our differences and varying viewpoints that made this country so truly great. What would they say about the party now?

With the rise of hate radio, media bullies, and Far Right groups, the environment has become constrained and narrow. These people are holding the party hostage, and always evoking the name Ronald Reagan, and claiming some kind of affiliation with his politics—and his ability to win elections. But Reagan did not win in 1981 because of the religious Right. He won with Democrats. He won with moderates. He won because his ideas were new and exciting—and appealed to a broad spectrum.

The bedrock of the Republican Party is freedom of the individual. Not groupthink. Not hatred. Not moral codes that we are supposed to live up to.

Goldwater and Reagan believed in freedom, true freedom, for all Americans to live out their lives in the way they choose. The way each American chooses, not their party, not their government, not a religious movement or an angry radio host.

You know, it's simple and powerful and beautiful. *You live your life and I'll live mine.* And I know in my heart that other members of my generation—a wonderful generation of enlightened souls—would feel energized and excited by these ideas if they were communicated properly, without dirty mudslinging and vicious venom, without unnecessary name-calling. Infused by new blood and new ideas, and new energy—optimism, not hate and negativity—the party could rise to prominence again. It would grow, expand, and become vital again.

I am not saying that we should abandon the core ideals that the Republican Party was built on. I am saying it is time to *remember them.*

It is time to return to honoring the individual. We need to make room for all Republicans. Today! Not tomorrow, but right now.

We shouldn't have to look a certain way, or live a certain way. That means that my gay friends, like Josh, shouldn't have to pretend they aren't gay—or have an unequal, Don't Ask, Don't Tell kind of lifestyle if they want to find a place in the Republican Party.

That means that my moderate friends shouldn't feel like outsiders. And my friends with tattoos and nose rings or women, like me, who like to wear leggings and not pantsuits—they shouldn't have to think twice about whether their bodies or clothing matched their political philosophy.

Being a Republican is not a lifestyle choice. And it doesn't mean you can't be young, or gay, or black, or anything else. It doesn't mean you listen to a certain kind of music or live in a certain kind of house.

And it shouldn't be controversial to be like me—a straight, pro-life Christian who is utterly determined to pass gay marriage in this country, who believes in a strong national defense, is worried about climate change, continues to support the wars in Iraq and Afghanistan, and who thinks government is best when it is efficient and accountable and stays out of people's lives and business.

There. I said it.

Those are my beliefs.

Do you think I should become a Democrat?

Of course not. In the last year, as a result of the campaign and what I learned, this is where my passion lies—and sense of purpose. I want to see if I can get the Republican Party to wake up.

Wake up!

Think for a moment about the negative voices that you hear on the radio and TV—on the Right and the Left. These people are selling hate and fear—and getting rich from it. These radio and TV stars care more about getting rich than they care about the future of this country, or the health of either political party. They make money by polarizing and spreading fear.

Think for a moment about the intolerant Far Right and its agenda. I am a passionate Christian, but I would never force my religious views on other individuals or want to see the agenda of the Republican Party narrowed to accommodate only one moral code. If the party continues to care only about these members, it will become smaller and smaller—and less relevant.

It is bad enough to find yourself put in a box by your opposition. But when a political party starts putting itself in a box, it is not a box. It is a coffin.

A new generation of Americans will be growing up and reaching political maturity in the next twenty years. And believe me, this amazing generation of passionate people—who were taught to volunteer, express their views, and pitch in—has more complicated views about church than it does about gays or premarital sex. This is why the party needs to wake up to gay marriage being a civil rights issue.

Wake up!

Wake up to new technology—the vast social networking sites like Facebook, MySpace, YouTube, and Twitter that have opened up a new world to those who weren't previously interested in politics. With the simple push of a button you can create a whole new movement with a whole new audience.

Wake up to the wonderful melting pot of America, where people of all colors and backgrounds and lifestyles are eager to connect with a political system that wants them, and speaks to them!

Wake up to the core ideal of the Republican Party—the freedom of the individual, the party of Abraham Lincoln—which brings us together more than it pulls us apart. We can disagree on all kinds of things, but we must stand together for equality, for freedom, for the ideals that make this country unique and great—and why so many people around the world dream of getting a chance to live here.

America is the home of the individual, where a woman like me can stop worrying about fitting in—and follow her passion instead.

Don't let me pick up this torch alone.

ACKNOWLEDGMENTS

I FEEL UNBELIEVABLY LUCKY TO HAVE GOTTEN A CHANCE to write this book. It couldn't have happened without the help and support of many people. First off, I'd like to thank my father's campaign staff, who devoted so many months and energy to a cause greater than themselves. To those staffers who are still speaking to me, and even those who aren't, I'd like to say thank you for inspiring and putting up with me.

Senator Joe Lieberman and Senator Lindsey Graham dispensed jokes and wisdom, and kept me in good spirits, throughout the campaign. I'd like to thank them for their acceptance and understanding and affection. Besides my dad, they are my two favorite men in politics. Flip Brophy saw potential in me when nobody else did—and made this book happen—for which I am so grateful. Flip, you are the Jewish mother I never had. Ellen Archer and Elizabeth Sabo at Hyperion gave me a great home in the book publishing world, and brought with them Kristin Kiser, Sarah Rucker, Marie Coolman, Christine Ragasa, and Laura Klynstra. I can't thank them all enough.

For the last eighteen months, Laurye Blackford has stuck with me through Twitter photo dramas and book deadline meltdowns. I want to thank her for helping me keep my life together, and for her advice and friendship. About those meltdowns . . . When I freaked out and thought I didn't know how to write a book, Martha Sherrill was there to tell me I could. Thank you for making this book a reality.

My friends are epically loyal, especially my Arizona girls. You know who you are, and you know I love you. Ramin Setoodeh, thank you for your amazing friendship and for reading this book in an early draft and offering great ideas and help. I'm grateful for my online followers for being supportive and keeping an open mind about politics. Bob Heckman and Leslee Sherrill gave me good advice and Stephen Talt offered support. Thank you.

I was lucky to have Adam Bonska photograph the book cover. He and his crew—Jeff Parshley and Chris Hayden—made the shoot a joy instead of a drain. Thanks also to Kari and Gary Johnson of Have Trunk, Will Travel and their sweet elephant, Tai. She was such a good sport.

My writing life began with the help of Shannon Bae and Heather Brand, who, along with Rob Kubasko, Melissa Shuffield, Frank La Rose, Claire Merkel, and Nancy Ives, nurtured and supported me every day of the campaign. It helped that my good friends Piper Baker and Josh Rupley were there to keep me, as if by magic, presentable. Meghan Latcovitch's loyalty to my family counts for a lot. After the election, Tina Brown, Edward Felsenthal and the Daily Beast gave me direction and gave my writing a home. Thank you for that.

Most of all, I'd like to thank my mom and dad for their love, inspiration, support, and for always letting me be me. They were okay when I said that I wanted to write a book, and they continued to offer support, even if they are sorry now. To Doug, Andy, Sidney, Jack, Jimmy, and Bridget—my brothers and sisters, my partners in crime—I love you so much, and thank you for your love and understanding.